NEO-ETHICAL LIVING

A Practical Guide to Success and Satisfaction

Arun Tiwari

celebrated co-author of *Wings of Fire*

Sakāl
Publications

Sakal Publications

NEO-ETHICAL LIVING

Sakal Media Pvt. Ltd.
595, Budhwar Peth,
Pune–411002, India

www.sakalmediagroup.com
sakalpublications.com
sakalprakashan@esakal.com

First Edition: October, 2025

ISBN: 978-93-49487-28-4

Cover Design: Rohit K.
Typesetting: MAP Systems, Bengaluru

Printed in India by Sakal Media Pvt. Ltd.

"Where there is righteousness in the heart,
There is beauty in the character.
When there is beauty in the character,
There is harmony in the home.
When there is harmony in the home,
There is order in the nation.
When there is order in the nation,
There is peace in the world."

— A. P. J. Abdul Kalam
11th President of India (1931–2015)

Contents

Introduction

There are moments when the world seems to tilt—when the noise of traffic fades, when the light falls in a certain way upon the floor, and one feels, not entirely at home, not entirely estranged, but suspended. In such moments, a question arises, fragile and insistent: *How should one live?* The old codes, carved in stone and whispered across centuries, stand like monuments in the distance—beautiful, solemn, but faint. Around us, the present hums with urgency: the phone vibrating, the schedules pressing, the mind fractured into a thousand fragments. What compass shall we hold, here and now, in this quickening age where speed outpaces reflection? It is not the ethics of the past alone that will guide us, but something reborn, renewed—what we might call "neo-ethical living."

English writer Virginia Woolf (1882–1941) reminds us, "Arrange whatever pieces come your way." Yet the act of arranging demands more than cleverness; it demands a rhythm, a harmony, a sense of purpose that rises from within. For life does not hand us a completed mosaic but a scattered collection of fragments—moments of joy, seasons of loss, shards of insight, stray encounters, sudden silences. To arrange them is not merely to put them in order, but to listen for the music they might make together, to sense the hidden pattern that memory, longing, and imagination trace across time. It is less the work of an engineer stacking bricks than of a weaver drawing threads into a fabric whose meaning emerges only when one steps back and sees the wholeness. And in that wholeness lies not perfection but coherence, a way of living where each piece, however uneven or unexpected, is welcomed into the larger design and given its place in the unfolding song.

This book is not a doctrine, nor a sermon. It is a walk through gardens of thought, through corridors of silence, through the inner chambers where conscience dwells. In its first part, we linger among Principles. We learn again to *feel yourself*—to notice the pulse of the inner world. We practice *emotional housekeeping*, sweeping clean the rooms of memory where clutter gathers, where sorrows linger too long. We stand in the *here and now*, that most elusive of places, and attempt to dwell there with presence. Gurudev Rabindranath Tagore (1861–1941) once said, "*The butterfly counts not months but moments, and has time enough.*" So too must we learn to live without haste, as though each moment were already whole.

We move beyond the small evasions—*going beyond avoidance*—and learn the quiet courage of facing life directly. And then, in gentle balance, we reflect on *self and others*, on the tender ties that bind us and the spaces that set us free. For, as Rumi whispers, "*A candle loses nothing by lighting another candle.*"

But principles alone are like stars—distant, glimmering, untouchable. We must bring them down into our hands, into the soil of living. Thus begins the second part: Practices. Here, we seek *inner peace*, not as escape but as stillness in the storm. We learn to *live spontaneously*, trusting the rhythm of life as one trusts the sea to hold the boat. We attempt to *access cosmic intelligence*—that vast web in which thought, breath, and being are not isolated but connected. We ground ourselves in *twenty timeless values*, those enduring companions of human dignity. And at last, we step into the *framework of neo-ethical living*, where the self is not diminished but enlarged by harmony—harmony with others, with nature, with the invisible order that sustains us.

Gurudev Tagore reminds us again: "*Faith is the bird that feels the light when the dawn is still dark.*" To live neo-ethically is to live in that faith—not as a possession of certainty, but as a movement through shadow with the assurance that light exists beyond our sight. It is a quiet rhythm of integrity, of care, of courage, carried even when the world confuses and tempts us with easier paths. To choose gentleness over aggression, responsibility over indifference, authenticity over pretence—these are the wing-beats of the bird sensing dawn. In such a life, one accepts the trembling half-light of confusion not as defeat, but as the soil where dignity takes root, where each act, however small, becomes a ripple towards the unseen horizon. And when morning comes, its brightness will not descend as a sudden miracle, but as the patient gathering of those countless choices made in darkness by souls who trusted the day.

This is no linear path, no ladder of rigid rungs. It is more like a spiral, or the turning of a tide, where motion is continuous yet never quite the same, where each return brings us to a higher or deeper place. One may begin anywhere—at stillness, at courage, at love—and be swept into the current of the whole, discovering that these qualities are not separate chambers but flowing rooms of the same house. The spiral teaches patience, for progress is not a march but a circling, not conquest but unfolding. Like the tide, it advances and recedes, drawing us back only to carry us further forward. In such a rhythm, there is no failure, only another curve of the journey, another chance to enter the circle from a different door and find that all doors, in time, open into the same vastness.

This is no linear path, no ladder of rigid rungs. It is more like a spiral, or the turning of a tide, where motion is continuous yet never quite the same, where each return brings us to a higher or deeper place. One may begin anywhere—at stillness, at courage, at love—and be swept into the current of the whole, discovering that these qualities are not separate chambers but flowing rooms of the same house. The spiral teaches patience, for progress is not a march but a circling, not conquest but unfolding. Like the tide, it advances and recedes, drawing us back only to carry us further forward. In such a rhythm, there is no failure, only another curve of the journey, another chance to enter the circle from a different door and find that all doors, in time, open into the same vastness.

To live neo-ethically is not to obey a list but to awaken a sensibility: to walk more slowly, to choose more carefully, to feel more deeply. It is to listen to the heart, to the other, to the faint music beneath the world. And so, dear reader, I invite you—read on, linger with these words, let them turn gently within you. For perhaps, in the end, the question is not How should one live? But how should one love?—and in answering that, you may discover both your purpose and your peace.

Arun Tiwari

Hyderabad
October 2025

Part I: Principles

In the rapidly evolving 21st-century landscape, ethics play a vital role in fostering a harmonious and conscientious society. Key principles guiding ethical behaviour include Feeling Yourself, Emotional Housekeeping, Living in the Here and Now, Going Beyond Avoidance, and Minding the Ease and Convenience of Others. Together, these principles guide individuals to live ethically in today's interconnected, fast-paced world by fostering self-awareness, emotional integrity, present-mindedness, courage, and compassion. Such an approach supports the development of a more empathetic, responsible, and resilient global society.

1

Feel Yourself

"Unexpressed emotions will never die. They are buried alive and will come forth later in uglier ways."

— Sigmund Freud
Austrian neurologist (1856–1939)

1. Emotions

A human being is a bundle of thoughts and feelings. Thoughts are what go on in one's mind, and emotions are what are felt by the body. While thoughts are straightforward—you know what you're thinking—emotions, on the other hand, are a combination of several components.

1.1 Subjective Experience

There is an internal sensation that accompanies an emotion. For example, happiness might feel like joy or contentment, while sadness might feel like heaviness or emptiness. Each person's experience of an emotion is unique.

1.2 Physiological Response

Bodily changes, such as increased heart rate, sweating, or changes in hormone levels, accompany emotions. For example, fear might trigger the "fight or flight" response, causing adrenaline to surge and preparing the body to react to danger.

1.3 Thought Response

This involves how we interpret and evaluate a situation, which in turn influences the emotion we feel. For example, if you perceive a situation as threatening, you might feel fear or anxiety. If you perceive it as rewarding, you might feel joy or excitement.

1.4 Behavioural Expression

Emotions often lead to outward expressions, such as facial expressions, body language, or actions. For example, anger might lead to a furrowed brow or raised voice, while happiness might lead to smiling or laughter.

Emotions are universal and innate, shared across cultures and species. American psychologist Paul Ekman (b. 1934) identified six basic emotions: happiness, sadness, fear, anger, surprise, and disgust. These emotions are considered "basic" because they are biologically hardwired and serve evolutionary functions. However, basic emotions seldom exist in their pure form and often manifest in more complex and nuanced ways. Jealousy, for example, is made of sadness, anger, and fear. Hate is a fusion of anger, fear, and disgust.

Emotions guide our choices by signalling what is important or valuable. For example, fear might lead us to avoid danger, while love might motivate us to care for others. Emotions enable us to convey our internal states to others, thereby fostering social bonds and promoting cooperation. For example, a smile can signal friendliness, while a frown can signal displeasure. Emotions drive us to act. For example, desire might motivate us to pursue a goal, while frustration might push us to find a solution to a problem.

2. Theories of Emotion

Emotions are multifaceted experiences that involve a combination of subjective feelings, physiological responses, cognitive processes, and behavioural expressions. They serve essential functions in our survival, decision-making, communication, and motivation. Understanding emotions can help us navigate our inner world and interactions with others more effectively.

2.1 James-Lange Theory

Developed by American philosopher John Dewey (1859–1952) and named for two scholars of his time, American philosopher William James (1842-1910) and Danish physician Carl Lange (1834–1900), this theory posits that emotions arise from physiological responses to stimuli. For example, you feel fear when your heart is racing.

2.2 Cannon-Bard Theory

Developed by American physiologist Walter Bradford Cannon (1871–1945), this concept proposes that emotions and physiological responses co-occur, rather than one causing the other. He coined the popular phrase "fight or flight response" to describe the body's reaction to a perceived harmful event, attack, or threat to survival, based on observation of animals.

2.3 Schachter-Singer Two-Factor Theory

American psychologists Stanley Schachter (1922–1997) and Jerome Singer (1934–2010) theorised that emotions result from both physiological arousal and mental appraisal. For example, you might feel fear because your heart is racing (physiological) and you interpret the situation as dangerous (cognitive). Imagine you're in a dark alley and hear footsteps behind you. Your heart starts racing (a physiological response to arousal). If you think someone is following you, you might interpret that arousal as fear. If you think it's a dog, you might interpret it as nervousness or even excitement. In essence, while physiological arousal provides the intensity of an emotion, our cognitive appraisal determines the specific type of emotion we feel.

2.4 Lazarus Cognitive Appraisal Theory

American psychologist Richard Lazarus (1922–2002) described the role of cognitive appraisal in determining emotional responses. It is not the event itself that causes the emotion, but rather how we understand it. Emotions are not simply automatic reactions to stimuli. How we interpret a situation plays a significant role in determining our emotional experience. A snarling dog might be perceived as a threat (leading to fear) or just a harmless animal (leading to no fear), depending on the context and our appraisal of the situation (e.g., if it's behind a fence).

2.5 Rope and Snake Analogy

The "rope-snake" analogy is a widely used and fundamental concept in Indian philosophy, particularly in Advaita Vedanta, to explain reality and the idea of illusion (maya). Like mistaking a rope for a snake in low light, ignorance can cause a distorted view of reality, while knowledge reveals the truth. The metaphor of mistaking a rope for a snake is very popular in India.

Rope represents the ultimate reality, Brahman, the unchanging, underlying truth of the universe. Snake represents the perceived world of multiplicity and diversity, which is a misinterpretation or illusion (maya) stemming from ignorance of Brahman's true nature. Mistaking the rope for a snake symbolises how the individual soul (Atman) misperceives the world due to ignorance (avidya), leading to fear and suffering.

Emotions are closely tied to the brain's limbic system, which comprises structures such as the amygdala, hippocampus, and hypothalamus. The amygdala plays a crucial role in processing emotions, such as fear and pleasure. The prefrontal cortex, which is involved in higher cognitive functions, also plays a role in regulating and interpreting emotions.

Emotions are central to mental health. Difficulty in experiencing, expressing, or regulating emotions can lead to mental health issues such as depression, anxiety, or personality disorders. Conversely, emotional intelligence—the ability to recognise, understand, and manage one's own emotions and those of others—is associated with better mental health and interpersonal relationships.

3. Unfelt Emotions

Human consciousness is a labyrinth—a winding maze of thoughts, memories, and emotions. Among these, unfelt emotions often dwell in the shadows, quietly influencing our choices, relationships, and even our identity. To acknowledge that we are, in essence, a repository of unfelt emotions is to confront the profound depth of human experience and the intricate ways we navigate through it. Some feelings are not consciously recognised or acknowledged by the individual. They may be buried deep, suppressed, or not noticed due to various factors, such as emotional coping mechanisms or a lack of awareness. American journalist and author Elizabeth Gilbert says, "Your emotions are the slaves to your thoughts, and you are the slave to your emotions".

3.1 The Nature of Unfelt Emotions

Unfelt emotions are not simply those suppressed by conscious will; they are often emotions we fail to recognise, process, or articulate. These feelings may arise from moments of trauma, unspoken desires, societal conditioning, or the overwhelming pace of modern life that leaves little room for introspection. They linger in the corners of our psyche, unnoticed but never inactive.

3.2 How They Manifest

These dormant emotions can often find expression in indirect ways—through physical ailments, mood swings, or behaviours that seem at odds with our rational selves. For instance, a persistent anxiety may stem from unresolved fears, while sudden irritability could be rooted in suppressed anger. In their silence, unfelt emotions are influential architects of our internal world.

3.3 Body Language and Tone of Voice

Subtle cues in body language, facial expressions, or vocal tone can reveal unspoken emotions, even if the person is not consciously aware of them. As goes a popular saying, "It's not what you say, but how you say it. Your tone of voice can convey emotions like happiness, sadness, anger, or sarcasm, even if your words don't explicitly express them".

4. Impact of Unfelt Emotions

Unfelt emotions act as invisible threads. They may manifest as misunderstandings or unspoken frustrations, creating distance where closeness is sought. When we carry unresolved sadness, disappointment, or resentment, it colours our interactions like a fog that we rarely see but often feel. Learning to identify and address these emotions is key to fostering deeper connections. Unfelt emotions can contribute to anxiety, depression, and other mental health challenges. Difficulty expressing emotions or misinterpreting others' emotional cues can strain relationships. A lack of awareness of one's emotional landscape can hinder personal growth and development. Unfelt emotions can create subtle barriers that prevent individuals from pursuing their goals or connecting authentically with others.

4.1 Psychological Impact

Over time, suppressing emotions can lead to a sense of emotional numbness or detachment, where individuals feel disconnected from their feelings. This can make it difficult to experience joy, love, or even sadness in a meaningful way. Unfelt emotions can contribute to mental health issues like anxiety and depression. When emotions are not processed, they can create internal tension and stress, leading to chronic worry, sadness, or feelings of emptiness.

Unfelt emotions can interfere with interpersonal relationships. If someone is unable to express or process their feelings, it can lead to misunderstandings, resentment, or emotional distance in relationships. Suppressed emotions can lead to distorted thinking patterns, such as catastrophising, overgeneralising, or black-and-white thinking. These cognitive distortions can further exacerbate emotional distress.

4.2 Physical Impact

Unfelt emotions can contribute to chronic stress, which has been linked to a range of physical health issues, including high blood pressure, heart disease, and weakened immune function. Unexpressed emotions can manifest as physical symptoms, including headaches, stomach aches, muscle tension, or fatigue. This is sometimes referred to as "somatisation," where emotional distress is expressed through the body. Suppressed emotions can lead to insomnia or other sleep disorders. The mind may continue to process unresolved emotions during sleep, leading to restless nights or nightmares.

4.3 Behavioural Impact

Unfelt emotions can lead to self-destructive behaviours and unhealthy coping mechanisms, such as substance abuse, overeating, or self-harm. These behaviours may provide temporary relief, but often exacerbate the underlying emotional issues. People who suppress emotions may avoid situations or relationships that could trigger those emotions. This can lead to social isolation or a narrowing of life experiences. When emotions are consistently suppressed, they may eventually erupt in unexpected and intense ways. For example, someone who has been bottling up anger might suddenly have an explosive outburst over a minor issue.

4.4 Impact on Self-Identity

Suppressing emotions can lead to a sense of inauthenticity, where individuals feel they are not being true to themselves. This can erode self-esteem and lead to feelings of emptiness or confusion about one's identity. Unfelt emotions can make it challenging to engage in meaningful self-reflection or personal growth. Without acknowledging and processing emotions, it's hard to learn from experiences or make positive changes.

4.5 Long-Term Consequences

Unfelt emotions can create a reservoir of unresolved pain that continues to affect an individual over time. This can lead to a sense of emotional heaviness or a feeling of being burdened. Unresolved emotions from past experiences can influence future relationships. For example, someone who has not processed feelings of betrayal may struggle to trust others in new relationships. When emotions are not processed, individuals may struggle to move forward in life, experiencing stagnation in emotional, social, or professional growth.

5. Coping with Unfelt Emotions

Unfelt emotions can have far-reaching impacts on mental, emotional, and physical well-being. While it may be tempting to suppress or ignore difficult emotions, doing so can lead to a host of negative consequences.

Acknowledging, expressing, and processing emotions is essential for emotional health and overall well-being. By finding healthy ways to address unexpressed emotions, individuals can reduce their impact and move toward a more balanced and fulfilling life.

5.1 Mindfulness and Awareness

Mindfulness involves paying attention to the present moment without judgment. It can help you become more aware of your emotions as they arise, rather than suppressing them. Techniques like meditation, deep breathing, or body scans can help you tune into your emotional state. Regularly check in with yourself to recognise and acknowledge your emotions. Ask yourself questions like, "What am I feeling right now?" or "What triggered this emotion?". This can help you become more attuned to your emotional landscape.

5.2 Yoga

Yoga and other somatic therapies focus on the connection between the mind and body, helping you release emotions that may be stored physically. Techniques like somatic experiencing or body-centred psychotherapy can be beneficial for processing unfelt emotions. Joining a support group or group therapy session can provide a sense of community and shared understanding. Hearing others' experiences can help you feel less alone and more validated in your emotional journey.

5.3 Creative Expression

Engaging in creative activities, such as drawing, painting, or sculpting, can provide a non-verbal outlet for expressing emotions. Art therapy can help you access and process emotions that may be difficult to articulate with words. Listening to or creating music, or engaging in dance, can help you connect with and release emotions. Movement and rhythm can be powerful tools for emotional expression. Creative writing can allow you to explore emotions safely and imaginatively. Writing poetry or fiction can help you externalise and process complex feelings.

5.4 Physical Activity

Physical activity, such as running or weightlifting, can help release pent-up emotions and reduce stress. Exercise also releases endorphins, which can improve mood and emotional well-being. Practices like boxing, karate, or jiu-jitsu can provide a physical outlet for emotions like anger or frustration, while also promoting discipline and focus. Dancing and singing are beneficial.

6. The 5-4-3-2-1 Technique

As a grounding exercise to stay present and manage overwhelming emotions, the 5-4-3-2-1 Technique is widely used. Its exact inventor remains unknown. The technique involves identifying five things you can see, four things you can touch, three things you can hear, two things you can smell, and one thing you can taste. By engaging your five senses to anchor you in the "here and now," it helps you manage anxiety, stress, or overwhelming emotions.

Very simply, find a quiet space, sit or stand in a comfortable position, and take a few deep breaths. Inhale deeply through your nose for a count of 4, hold for 4, and exhale through your mouth for a count of 6. Look around and notice five things you can see. They can be big or small, near or far. Now, notice four things you can feel with your sense of touch, listen for three sounds you can hear, identify two things you can smell, for example, the scent of fresh coffee, and taste, for example, a sip of water. You should feel more grounded and present in the moment. If you're still feeling anxious, you can repeat the exercise or focus on your breathing for a few more moments.

By focusing on your senses, you redirect your attention away from anxious thoughts or overwhelming emotions. It reduces feelings of dissociation or being "stuck in your head". Engaging your senses can help activate the parasympathetic nervous system, which promotes relaxation and reduces the "fight or flight" response. The more you use this technique, the more effective it becomes. By engaging your five senses, you can calm your mind, reduce emotional intensity, and feel more connected to your surroundings anytime, anywhere.

7. Connecting with Others

Human beings are inherently social creatures, and meaningful relationships provide emotional support, reduce stress, and foster a sense of belonging. No wonder unfelt emotions ripple through society. Cultural norms often dictate which emotions are acceptable to display, thereby shaping collective repositories of unacknowledged feelings. Historical injustices, social inequalities, and communal traumas usually persist in the form of unacknowledged societal emotions, perpetuating cycles that remain unbroken until they are consciously addressed.

Connecting with others is a fundamental aspect of emotional health and well-being. Sharing your emotions with someone you trust can help you feel less isolated and more supported. Sometimes, simply talking about what you're feeling can help you better understand and process it. Support groups, whether in-person or online, can provide a sense of community and shared understanding. Hearing others' experiences can help you feel less alone and more validated in your emotional journey.

Regularly check in with friends, family, and loved ones. Simple gestures, such as a phone call, a text message, or spending quality time together, can strengthen bonds. Show appreciation for the people in your life. Expressing gratitude can deepen connections and improve mutual feelings of positivity. When interacting with others, practice active listening and be fully present. Open up to trusted friends or family members about your emotions.

Sharing your thoughts and feelings can provide relief and help you gain perspective. Don't hesitate to ask for support when you need it. Whether it's emotional support or practical assistance, reaching out can strengthen relationships and alleviate stress. Volunteering for a cause you care about can provide a sense of purpose and connect you with like-minded individuals. Try to attend social gatherings, even if it's outside your comfort zone. These events can provide opportunities to meet new people and strengthen existing relationships.

8. Setting Boundaries

Setting boundaries is crucial for maintaining emotional health and fostering healthy relationships. Boundaries help you define what is acceptable and unacceptable in your interactions with others, protecting your emotional well-being and ensuring that your needs are respected. Here's a comprehensive guide to setting and maintaining healthy boundaries for emotional health:

8.1 Understand Boundaries

Emotional boundaries involve protecting your feelings and emotional energy. They help you decide how much emotional labour you're willing to take on and how much you're eager to share with others. Physical boundaries pertain to your personal space and the extent of physical touch. They help you feel comfortable and safe in your interactions. Time boundaries involve managing your time and energy. They help you prioritise your needs and avoid overcommitting.

Material boundaries relate to your possessions and resources. They allow you to decide what you're willing to share or lend to others. Mental boundaries involve protecting your thoughts, beliefs, and opinions. They help you maintain your individuality and avoid being overly influenced by others.

8.2 Identify Your Needs and Limits

Take time to reflect on your emotional needs, values, and limits. Consider what makes you feel comfortable, respected, and fulfilled. Identify situations or interactions that drain your energy or cause emotional distress. These are areas where you may need to set boundaries. Understand that setting boundaries is a form of self-care. It's about protecting your emotional health and ensuring you have the energy to care for yourself and others. Hong Kong-American martial artist Bruce Lee famously said, "If you always put a limit on everything you do, physical or anything else. It will permeate your work and your life. There are no limits. There are only plateaus, and you must not stay there; you must go beyond them".

8.3 Communicate and Enforce Your Boundaries

Clearly define what your boundaries are. For example, if you need time to yourself after work, specify that you're unavailable for calls or visits during that time. Communicate your boundaries calmly and confidently. Avoid being defensive or apologetic, as this can undermine your message. Consistently enforce your boundaries to show that they are essential and non-negotiable. Inconsistency can lead to confusion and boundary violations. It's okay to say no to requests or demands that cross your boundaries. Saying no is a way of respecting your own needs and limits. If someone crosses your boundaries, address it promptly and assertively. Reiterate your boundaries and explain why they are essential to you. Equally important is to avoid pressuring others to change their boundaries or do things they're uncomfortable with. Respect their limits as you would want them to respect yours.

8.4 Be Kind to Yourself

It's common to feel guilty when setting boundaries, but remember that taking care of yourself is not selfish. Let go of guilt and focus on the positive impact of your boundaries. Adjust boundaries as needed. Your needs and limits may change over time, so it's essential to re-evaluate and adjust your boundaries regularly. However, setting boundaries inevitably leads to conflict, but it is necessary to prioritise your emotional health. Practice self-compassion and remind yourself that boundaries are essential for your well-being.

9. Summary

To be human is to be in constant dialogue with oneself, navigating waters both calm and turbulent. Unfelt emotions, while invisible, shape the contours of this journey. In embracing them, we do not merely feel; we evolve. For within these silent forces lies the essence of what it means to live authentically and expansively. Experiencing and processing your emotions, including those that are uncomfortable or negative, is crucial for both mental and physical health. Suppressing or avoiding emotions can lead to various health issues, while accepting and processing them can improve overall well-being.

2

Emotional Housekeeping

"Until you make the unconscious conscious, it will direct your life and you will call it fate."

—Carl Jung

Swiss psychiatrist (1875–1961)

1. Stored-up Emotions

Emotions are a vital part of the human experience, yet they sometimes accumulate like unaddressed clutter in our minds. Pent-up emotions can weigh us down, affecting our relationships, productivity, and mental health. By taking stock of these emotions and engaging in emotional housekeeping, we can cultivate clarity, resilience, and inner peace.

Pent-up emotions are feelings that have been suppressed, ignored, or left unprocessed over time. They often stem from stress, unresolved conflicts, traumatic experiences, or the daily challenges of life. These emotions may manifest as physical tension, mood swings, exhaustion, or even difficulty concentrating. Taking stock of your emotions involves recognising and understanding what you're feeling.

2. Name Your Emotion

Labelling your emotions can be surprisingly powerful. Ask yourself, "What am I feeling right now?" and put words to your sensations—whether it's sadness, anger, joy, fear, or confusion. There are various ways emotions are named, and they vary across languages. Even the six universal basic emotions are called differently by different people.

Happiness is also felt as joy, contentment, and satisfaction. Sadness is called grief, sorrow, or disappointment. Anger is often perceived as frustration, irritation, or rage; fear is typically associated with anxiety, nervousness, or terror; surprise is frequently expressed as shock or astonishment; and disgust is commonly understood as revulsion, distaste, or aversion.

Then there are subtle or nuanced emotions. Longing for the past is nostalgia. Interest and inquisitiveness are felt as curiosity. Openness and exposure are felt as vulnerability. Resentment is bitterness and indignation. Relief is the ease and comfort that follows stress. Despair is hopelessness or despondency. Extreme happiness, elation, is euphoria. Pensive sadness is melancholy. Deep longing, desire is yearning. Above all, there is ambivalence, characterised by mixed feelings and uncertainty. The point is that giving a name to what you are feeling is very important.

Identifying and naming an emotion helps you understand what you're feeling. This clarity can help reduce confusion and make sense of your internal experience. Naming emotions encourages you to reflect on why you're feeling a certain way, which can lead to deeper self-awareness and personal growth. Once you name an emotion, it becomes easier to manage. For example, recognising that you're feeling "frustrated" rather than just "bad" allows you to take specific steps to address the frustration. Simply labelling an emotion can reduce its intensity. Research shows that putting feelings into words can calm the brain's emotional centres (like the amygdala) and help you regain control.

2.1 Reflect on Their Origins

Once you've identified your emotions, delve deeper to uncover their sources. Are they tied to a past event, a current challenge, or recurring worries?. Pinpointing the root of your emotions can help you gain insight into your patterns and triggers.

2.2 Accept and Validate Your Feelings

Remember that all emotions are valid. There's no "wrong" way to feel. Acknowledging your feelings without shame or guilt is an essential step toward healing. Instead of dismissing or minimising what you're experiencing, embrace it as part of your humanity.

3. Clearing the Clutter

Once you've named your emotions, it's time to engage in emotional housekeeping. Think of this as tidying up your inner world to create space for growth and positivity.

3.1 Acknowledge Your Emotion

Identify what you're feeling and name the emotions you're experiencing. Are you feeling anger, sadness, guilt, or anxiety? Avoid suppressing or denying your feelings. Acceptance is key to processing and releasing them.

3.2 Express the Emotion

Unexpressed feelings can become stagnant. Find healthy outlets to release them—whether through journaling, talking to a trusted friend, creating art, or engaging in physical activity like dancing or exercising. Expression allows your emotions to flow and dissipate.

3.3 Describe the Cause

Explain what triggered the emotion. For example, "I'm grateful because my friends helped me". Talk about how the emotion affects you. For example, "Their support made me feel less alone". Use 'I' Statements: Focus on your own experience. Like, 'I feel happy when..."

3.4 Let Go of What You Can't Control

Focus on the Present: Worrying about the past or future can create emotional clutter. Practice mindfulness to stay grounded in the present moment.

Release Control: Accept that there are things beyond your control. Letting go of the need to control everything can free you from unnecessary stress and anxiety.

4. Cultivate Gratitude

Gratitude is the practice of recognising and appreciating the positive aspects of life, whether they come from others, the world around us, or within ourselves. It involves acknowledging the good things we have, the kindness we receive, and the blessings we often overlook. Gratitude is not just a fleeting feeling of thankfulness; it's a deeper, more intentional attitude that can transform how we perceive and interact with the world.

Gratitude shifts your focus from what's troubling you to what enriches your life. Make a habit of acknowledging the things, people, and experiences that bring you joy. This practice helps you rewire your mind to cultivate a more positive outlook.

Improves Mental Health: Studies have shown that gratitude can reduce stress, anxiety, and depression while increasing overall happiness and life satisfaction. Expressing gratitude can deepen connections with others, fostering a sense of mutual appreciation and support. Gratitude helps us focus on what we have rather than what we lack, making it easier to cope with challenges and setbacks. Grateful people tend to take better care of themselves, resulting in improved physical health and overall well-being.

When faced with challenges, try to find the silver lining. Ask yourself, "What can I learn from this?" or "How has this situation made me stronger?". Reframe negative thoughts by focusing on what you still have rather than what you've lost. Start or end your day with a gratitude practice. For example, you can offer a prayer of thanks, express gratitude to a loved one, or take a moment to reflect on your blessings. Gratitude doesn't always have to be about significant events or achievements. Appreciate the small, everyday moments—like a warm cup of coffee, a smile from a stranger, or a quiet moment of peace.

Gratitude is a skill that can be developed with practice. By making it a regular part of your life, you can shift your mindset to one of abundance and positivity, leading to greater happiness and fulfilment. Start small, be consistent, and watch how gratitude transforms your outlook and relationships. Cultivate a habit of not comparing yourself to others, as this can lead to feelings of inadequacy or envy. Instead, focus on your journey and what you're grateful for in your life. French author Marcel Proust (1871–1922) wrote, "Let us be grateful to the people who make us happy; they are the charming gardeners who make our souls blossom".

5. Cultivate Patience

Patience is the ability to remain calm and composed in the face of delays, challenges, or frustrations. American author, Arnold H. Glasow (1905–1997), so aptly said, "The key to everything is patience. You get the chicken by hatching the egg, not by smashing it". It's a valuable skill that can improve your mental well-being, relationships, and overall quality of life. Here are practical strategies to cultivate patience:

5.1 Understand the Nature of Patience

Recognise that patience isn't something you're born with—it's a skill that can be developed with practice. Understand that life is unpredictable, and not everything will go as planned. Accepting this reality can help you release frustration. Embrace the unpredictability of life, for sometimes the detours lead us to the most beautiful destinations beyond our plans. The occurrence of events by chance, happily or beneficially, is well known. Many unexpected discoveries or moments of luck have occurred seemingly by accident, yet they bring about positive outcomes. Alexander Fleming accidentally discovered penicillin in 1928 when mould grew in his petri dish and killed bacteria, which is perhaps the best known.

5.2 Shift Your Perspective

Instead of viewing a delay as a waste of time, see it as an opportunity to pause, reflect, or practice patience. Remind yourself that many things in life take time to unfold. A long-term perspective can help you remain patient with processes such as personal growth, career development, or relationships. Thomas A. Edison (1847–1931) has famously said, "Many of life's failures are people who did not realise how close they were to success when they gave up".

5.3 Set Realistic Expectations

Unrealistic expectations often lead to impatience. Set achievable goals and understand that progress takes time. When planning, factor in potential delays (such as traffic or slow service) so you're not caught off guard. There is an anonymous quote, "Live your life, not to impress others, but to be your best self. Don't set expectations that are too high or too low—they should be realistic".

6. Examine Your Impatience

American novelist Joyce Meyer (b. 1943) writes, "Patience is not the ability to wait, but the ability to keep a good attitude while waiting". Impatience is often seen as a negative trait, but it can also be a productive attitude and a valuable teacher if approached with the right mindset. Impatience arises when we feel frustrated by delays, obstacles, or unmet expectations. Instead of letting impatience create stress or rash decisions, we can use it as an opportunity for self-reflection, growth, and improvement.

6.1 Identify the Root of Your Impatience

Often, impatience stems from a desire for control or fear of uncertainty. Understanding the underlying cause can help you address it more effectively. Ask yourself: Why am I feeling impatient? Is it because you're in a hurry, feeling overwhelmed, or worried about missing an opportunity?. Genevan philosopher Jean-Jacques Rousseau (1712–1778) declared, "Patience is bitter, but its fruit is sweet".

6.2 Practice Self-Awareness

Impatience can be a signal that you're out of alignment with your values or goals. For example, if you're impatient with a slow-moving project, it might indicate that you're not fully engaged or that the project doesn't align with your priorities. Use impatience as a cue to reflect on what truly matters to you and whether you're spending your time and energy in meaningful ways.

6.3 Reframe Impatience as a Desire for Progress

Impatience can be a sign that you're eager to achieve something or make progress. Instead of letting it frustrate you, channel that energy into productive action. For example, if you're impatient about a slow career trajectory, use that feeling as motivation to set clear goals, seek mentorship, or acquire new skills. As goes one proverb, "Impatience is a form of weakness; patience is a form of strength".

6.4 Use Impatience as a Catalyst for Change

If you're consistently impatient in a particular area of your life, it might be a sign that something needs to change. For example, if you're impatient with your job, it may be a sign that it's time to explore new opportunities or consider alternative career paths. Use impatience as a motivator to make positive changes rather than staying stuck in a frustrating situation.

Impatience is a natural human emotion, but it doesn't have to control you. American poetess Marianne Moore (1887-1972) wrote, "Impatience is the mark of independence, not of bondage". By reflecting on the root causes of your impatience and using it as a tool for self-awareness and growth, you can transform it into a positive force. Whether it's learning to let go of control, setting realistic expectations, or embracing the process, impatience can teach you valuable lessons about yourself and how you approach life. With practice, you can cultivate greater patience, resilience, and a deeper appreciation for the journey.

7. Cultivate a Growth Mindset

A growth mindset is a concept developed by American psychologist Carol Dweck (b. 1946) for the belief that abilities, intelligence, and talents can be developed through effort, learning, and persistence. People with a growth mindset see challenges as opportunities to grow, embrace learning, and believe that their potential is not fixed but can be expanded over time. It contrasts with a fixed mindset, which holds that abilities and intelligence are static traits that cannot be significantly changed.

The Growth mindset implies seeing challenges as opportunities to learn and grow, rather than as threats or obstacles, and recognising that effort and hard work are crucial for achieving mastery and improvement. It also involves viewing feedback and criticism as valuable tools for growth, rather than as personal attacks. Feeling motivated by the success of others rather than being threatened or jealous, and valuing the learning process and effort over immediate results or innate talent, individuals with a growth mindset bounce back from setbacks and failures with a positive attitude and a willingness to try again.

7.1 How to Develop a Growth Mindset

Developing a growth mindset is a gradual process that involves changing the way you think about learning, effort, and failure. Here are some practical steps to cultivate a growth mindset: Recognise that no one is perfect, and mistakes are a natural part of the learning process. Instead of hiding your flaws, view them as opportunities for improvement.

7.2 View Challenges as Opportunities

Shift your perspective on challenges. Instead of avoiding them, see them as chances to learn and grow. Remind yourself that struggling with something difficult means you're expanding your abilities. Reframe failure as a stepping stone to success. Instead of thinking, "I failed," believe, "I learned something valuable".

7.3 Value Effort Over Talent

Recognise that effort and hard work are more important than innate talent. Celebrate the process of learning and the effort you put in, even if the results aren't immediate. When you encounter a task you can't do, add the word "yet" to your thinking. For example, "I can't solve this problem yet". This simple shift in language reinforces the idea that you're on a learning journey and that improvement is possible.

A growth mindset is a powerful way of thinking that can transform how you approach challenges, failures, and learning opportunities. By believing in your ability to grow and improve, you can unlock your potential and achieve greater success in all areas of life. Individuals with a growth mindset are better equipped to handle setbacks and recover from failure. By embracing challenges and persisting through difficulties, individuals with a growth mindset often achieve higher levels of success. Cultivating a growth mindset takes time and practice, but the benefits are well worth the effort.

8. Indulge in Self-Care

Taking care of your physical, mental, and emotional health is vital for maintaining balance. Prioritise restful sleep, nourishing food, regular exercise, and relaxation. Activities such as meditation, yoga, or spending time in nature can significantly boost your mood.

Self-care is the practice of taking intentional actions to nurture your physical, mental, emotional, and spiritual well-being. It's about prioritising your needs and making time for activities that replenish your energy and help you feel balanced and fulfilled. Self-care is not selfish—it's essential for maintaining your health and resilience, especially in the face of life's challenges.

8.1 Physical Self-Care

Get Enough Sleep: Aim for 8 hours of quality sleep each night. Establish a calming bedtime routine to help you unwind. Fuel your body with balanced meals that include fruits, vegetables, lean proteins, and whole grains. Stay hydrated by drinking plenty of water. Engage in physical activities you enjoy, such as walking, yoga, dancing, or cycling. Exercise boosts your mood and energy levels. Take time to care for your body, whether it's a relaxing bath, a skincare routine, or grooming habits that make you feel good.

8.2 Mental Self-Care

Limit Information Overload. Reduce exposure to negative news or social media that can overwhelm your mind. Set boundaries for screen time. Spend time on activities that bring you joy and stimulate your mind, such as reading, painting, puzzles, or playing music. Challenge your brain by learning a new skill, language, or hobby. This can boost your confidence and keep your mind sharp.

8.3 Social Self-Care

Connect with Loved Ones. Spend quality time with family and friends who uplift and support you. Nurture meaningful relationships. Engage in groups or activities where you can connect with like-minded people, such as clubs, classes, or volunteer organisations. Distance yourself from people who drain your energy or bring negativity into your life. Express appreciation for the people in your life. A simple thank-you or heartfelt message can strengthen your connections.

8.4 Spiritual Self-Care

Meditate or Pray. Engage in practices that help you connect with your inner self or a higher power. Meditation, prayer, or mindfulness can provide a sense of peace and purpose. Spend Time in Nature. Take walks in the park, hike, or sit outside to connect with the natural world. Nature can be deeply grounding and rejuvenating. Organise your workspaces to create a sense of order and calm.

8.5 Creative Self-Care

Engage in Art. Express yourself through creative outlets, such as painting, drawing, writing, or crafting. Creativity can be a powerful tool for processing emotions and relaxation. Create playlists that match your mood or help you unwind. Music can be a great source of comfort and inspiration. Let go of inhibitions and dance to your favourite songs. Movement can be a fun and liberating form of self-expression. Do something spontaneous. Break out of your routine and try something new or unexpected. Spontaneity can bring joy and excitement to your life.

Self-care is a personal and ongoing practice that looks different for everyone. The key is to listen to your needs and make time for activities that nourish your mind, body, and soul. Remember, self-care isn't a luxury—it's a necessity for maintaining your well-being and resilience. Start small, be consistent, and prioritise yourself. Over time, you'll notice the positive impact self-care has on your overall quality of life. Remember the famous words of American novelist Eleanor Brown (b. 1973), "Rest and self-care are so important. When you take time to replenish your spirit, it allows you to serve others from a place of overflow. You cannot serve from an empty vessel".

9. Summary

Taking stock of pent-up emotions and engaging in emotional housekeeping is an ongoing journey rather than a one-time task. Just as you periodically clean your physical environment, tending to your emotional well-being requires regular attention and care. By embracing your feelings, expressing them constructively, and nurturing yourself, you can create a harmonious and fulfilling inner world.

3

Live Here and Now

"Realise deeply that the present moment is all you ever have.
Make the Now the primary focus of your life."

—Eckhart Tolle

German-born spiritual teacher (b. 1948)

1. Embracing the Present

The question of whether one should live for the promise of a better afterlife while enduring the imperfections of present existence is as old as human consciousness itself. It touches upon the core of existential philosophy, spirituality, and our understanding of purpose within the framework of our mortal journey. This belief often provides a sense of purpose, reminding individuals that the struggles they endure now are not in vain but are preparatory steps for a higher existence. It fosters resilience in the face of adversity and encourages adherence to moral codes and spiritual practices.

However, living solely for an afterlife can sometimes lead to neglect of the present. Young people are not at all convinced. The inadequacies and sufferings of life—poverty, injustice, and loneliness—can become overshadowed and dismissed as mere tests or transitory inconveniences, rather than challenges to be actively addressed and resolved. When one fixates on an intangible future, there is the risk of losing sight of the tangible reality at hand, including relationships, opportunities, and personal growth. Furthermore, this focus on an afterlife has historically been exploited to justify societal inequities, with the promise of future rewards used to placate those suffering oppression or deprivation. It can create an imbalance wherein the pursuit of fulfilment in this life is seen as selfish or unworthy in contrast to the spiritual rewards of another realm. Is it possible to reconcile the desire for a better afterlife with the pursuit of a meaningful present? Why not live with the awareness of a future existence, while actively seeking to improve the circumstances of one's current life?

2. Finding Fulfilment in the Now

Ultimately, the present moment is the only reality we can truly grasp. Philosophers like Eckhart Tolle and spiritual traditions such as Zen Buddhism encourage individuals to focus on the "now", arguing that joy and contentment stem not from the promise of distant rewards but from mindful engagement with life as it unfolds. By acknowledging inadequacies yet striving for growth and connection, one can transform suffering into opportunity and inadequacy into a springboard for resilience. In this sense, the idea of a better afterlife becomes less a distant mirage and more a mirror reflecting the values we cultivate in the present. Living for both realms—for the eternal and the present—is a delicate dance that requires introspection, balance, and an unwavering commitment to authenticity–the dynamic interplay between hope and action, faith and reality. While the promise of a better beyond can inspire, it is the richness of the present—the choices we make, the love we share, and the courage we show—that defines the essence of our humanity. The richness of the present moment lies in its immediacy, depth, and potential.

2.1 Being Fully Present

Being fully present allows you to experience life as it unfolds, without the distractions of past regrets or future anxieties. This heightened awareness can reveal subtle details and beauty that might otherwise go unnoticed.

2.2 Connection

The present moment is where genuine connection happens—whether with others, nature, or yourself. It's in the "now" that you can truly listen, feel, and engage.

2.3 Freedom

The present is free from the burdens of the past and the uncertainties of the future. It's a space where you can act, create, and choose without being weighed down by what has been or what might be.

2.4 Potential

Every moment holds infinite possibilities. The decisions you make, the actions you take, and the thoughts you nurture in the present shape your future. It's a fertile ground for growth and transformation. According to Buddhist monk Thich Nhat Hanh, "The present moment is filled with joy and happiness. If you are attentive, you will see it."

3. Let Go of the Past and Future

The past is gone, and the future is uncertain. Dwelling on them can rob you of the joy of the present. When you catch yourself ruminating on the past or worrying about the future, remind yourself that the only moment you have control over is now. Letting go of what you can't change frees you to focus on what you can—your actions and attitudes in the present.

Overthinking past mistakes or regrets only keeps you stuck in a cycle of guilt or sadness. Acceptance is the first step toward letting go. For example, instead of saying, "I should have done better," try, "I did the best I could with what I knew at the time." Instead of dwelling on past mistakes, focus on the lessons they've taught you. Use those lessons to make better choices in the present. For example, if a past relationship failed, reflect on what you learned about communication or boundaries.

3.1 The Weight of the Past

The past is a landscape of memories, triumphs, and regrets. While it offers valuable lessons and shapes parts of who we are, it can also become a heavy weight if allowed to dominate our thoughts and emotions. Dwelling on past failures, lost opportunities, or painful experiences often traps us in cycles of self-criticism and yearning for what cannot be undone. The past is unchangeable, and clinging to it only deepens emotional scars rather than healing them.

3.2 The Anxiety of the Future:

Overthinking about the future pulls us away from the present. We plan and strategise endlessly, trying to anticipate every possible scenario, yet life remains unpredictable. This focus on the "what-ifs" and "maybes" steals our peace and prevents us from appreciating the moments unfolding before us. Learning to accept uncertainty is a cornerstone of letting go of future anxieties.

4. Set Intentions, Not Expectations

Setting intentions rather than focusing on expectations is a decisive mindset shift that can lead to greater peace, fulfilment, and alignment with your true self. It's okay to have goals, but don't let them consume you—set intentions for how you want to live today, rather than obsessing over future outcomes. For example, instead of worrying about whether you'll achieve a big goal, focus on taking small, meaningful steps today. It means aligning your actions with your values and purpose. When you live in alignment with your values, you're more likely to feel fulfilled, even in the smallest moments.

Intentions matter more than expectations. Intentions are about how you want to show up and act in the present moment. They are focused on the present moment, which is the only thing you can control. Expectations are often tied to specific outcomes, which are outside your control. When those outcomes don't happen, it can lead to frustration or disappointment. For example, if you expect a friend to act a certain way and they don't, you may feel let down. But if you set an intention to be kind and understanding, you'll feel more at peace regardless of their actions.

Intentions allow you to adapt and grow, even when things don't go as planned. They encourage you to focus on your actions and mindset, rather than external results. If you set an intention to stay curious and learn, you'll grow from every experience, even if it's not what you initially expected. Intentions are often tied to your core values and purpose, helping you live a more meaningful and authentic life.

4.1 Focus on the Process, Not the Outcome

Instead of fixating on a specific result, focus on the steps you can take today to move in the direction you want. For example, instead of expecting to lose 5 kg, set an intention to eat mindfully and move your body daily. Intentions are about how you want to act or feel in the present moment. Ask yourself, "How do I want to show up today?" By focusing on what you can control (your actions and mindset), you'll feel less anxious about outcomes.

4.2 Release Attachment to Results

While it's okay to have goals, don't let them define your happiness. Focus on the effort and energy you put in, rather than the outcome. For example, if you're working on a project, set an intention to give it your best effort, rather than expecting it to be perfect or successful. Don't say, "I expect never to make mistakes." Say instead, "I intend to learn from my mistakes and grow." Instead of saying, "I expect to feel confident in every situation," say that "I intend to show up authentically, even when I feel uncertain." Intentions help you stay grounded and adaptable, even when things don't go as planned. Intentions are about how you want to live and who you want to be, while expectations are often tied to specific outcomes that are outside your control. By setting intentions, you empower yourself to focus on the present moment, align with your values, and cultivate a sense of peace and fulfilment, no matter what happens. Remember, life is a journey, not a destination. Intentions help you enjoy the ride.

5. Finding Strength in the Unknown

Uncertainty is an intrinsic part of life—a constant companion that shapes our experiences, challenges our perspectives, and encourages growth. While the unknown can often evoke feelings of discomfort, fear, or hesitation, it is in these very moments of uncertainty that opportunities for transformation and triumph emerge. To embrace uncertainty is to accept its presence as a catalyst for evolving into a more resilient, adaptive, and insightful individual.

5.1 The Nature of Uncertainty

Uncertainty is not merely a lack of clarity or foresight; it is the space where possibilities reside. It exists in the gaps between the predictable and unpredictable, where plans can falter but creativity can thrive. Modern society often glorifies control and meticulous planning, yet actual growth usually arises from the courage to step into the unknown and navigate its complexities. This natural inclination toward certainty can make uncertainty seem like an unwelcome disruption. It challenges our sense of control and forces us to confront risks, which can trigger anxiety and stress. However, it is essential to recognise that uncertainty is not inherently harmful; it is a condition that carries both challenges and potential rewards.

5.2 The Power of Embracing Uncertainty

When we learn to embrace uncertainty rather than resist it, we open ourselves to a world of possibilities. It empowers us to lean into discomfort, adapt to change, and cultivate resilience. History is replete with examples of individuals and societies that have thrived in the face of unpredictability, turning adversity into innovation and setbacks into stepping stones.

5.3 Uncertainty as a Driver of Growth

Embracing uncertainty often requires stepping out of our comfort zones, which is a key ingredient for personal development. It challenges us to re-evaluate assumptions, build mental flexibility, and sharpen our problem-solving skills. Many groundbreaking ideas and discoveries arise from uncertain situations. Uncertainty invites experimentation and collaboration, sparking creativity that flourishes when boundaries are undefined. Learning to navigate uncertainty strengthens our ability to adapt to changing circumstances. It teaches us to trust ourselves, embrace imperfection, and build resilience in the face of setbacks.

5.4 Focus on What You Can Control

While uncertainty often emphasises the unknown, it is helpful to redirect your attention to areas where you have influence. Identifying small, actionable steps can restore a sense of agency and reduce feelings of helplessness. In many ways, uncertainty is a mirror that reflects our inner strengths and vulnerabilities. A life filled with certainty may offer comfort, but a life that embraces uncertainty often leads to greater richness, meaning, and fulfilment. From making career changes to embarking on new relationships, uncertainty pervades the decisions we face daily. These moments of the unknown, though daunting, also hold the promise of transformation. By embracing uncertainty, we seize the opportunity to learn, adapt, and grow.

To embrace uncertainty is to embrace life in its entirety—its challenges, surprises, and infinite potential. It is a skill that requires practice, courage, and self-confidence. Though the unknown may seem intimidating, it is often where we find the richest experiences and the most profound insights. By stepping into the uncertainty with openness and determination, we unlock the door to a future filled with possibility and promise.

6. Focused and Purposeful Living

In a world brimming with distractions, the ability to engage fully in what you're doing has become an exceptional skill. Whether it's completing a work task, enjoying a hobby, or simply savouring a quiet moment, the art of deep focus can transform mundane activities into meaningful experiences. But why is full engagement so critical, and how can we cultivate it in a society that thrives on multitasking and instant gratification?

Engaging fully in an activity is not merely about concentration; it is about immersing yourself in the present moment and giving your undivided attention to what lies before you. This practice offers numerous benefits that permeate every aspect of life. When you commit fully to one task, your efficiency skyrockets. Dividing your attention among multiple tasks often leads to errors and wasted time. On the other hand, focusing entirely on one endeavour allows you to complete it with care and precision.

Full engagement fosters an environment where creativity can flourish. By immersing yourself in the process, you enable your mind to explore new ideas and solutions without the interference of external distractions. Giving your undivided attention to conversations and interactions strengthens bonds with others. People feel valued and appreciated when they notice you listening actively and participating wholeheartedly. According to William James, "The most basic of all human needs is the need to be appreciated and understood."

6.1 Barriers to Full Engagement

Despite its evident benefits, achieving full engagement can be challenging. Identifying the obstacles that hinder your focus is the first step to overcoming them. The omnipresence of smartphones, notifications, and social media is one of the greatest threats to focused living. The constant interruption of alerts pulls you away from the task at hand, fragmenting your attention. Many believe that multitasking is a sign of productivity, but it dilutes your attention and leads to mediocre results. The human brain is not designed to perform multiple complex tasks simultaneously with high efficiency. Mental clutter from stress or information overload can make it difficult to focus. A restless mind struggles to settle into the present moment, leaving you disengaged from your activities. Create a minimalist environment that supports concentration. Turn off unnecessary notifications, de-clutter your workspace, and set boundaries with people and technology during focus time.

6.2 Lack of Purpose

When an activity lacks meaning or purpose, it becomes harder to engage fully. Without a connection to the task, you may find your thoughts wandering or your interest waning. Achieving full engagement requires deliberate practice and a willingness to make mindful choices. Here are strategies to help you immerse yourself in what you're doing. Clarify your goals before beginning an activity. Ask yourself what you hope to accomplish and why it matters. Having clear intentions keeps you motivated and aligned with your purpose. Overwhelming tasks can lead to procrastination and disengagement. Divide large projects into smaller, actionable steps to maintain momentum and focus.

6.3 Adopt the Flow State

The "flow state", coined by Hungarian-American psychologist Mihaly Csikszentmihalyi, occurs when you are completely absorbed in an activity that challenges you while matching your skill level. Seek activities that inspire this harmonious balance. Immerse yourself in the sensory aspects of an activity. Whether it's the texture of a brushstroke, the rhythm of a song, or the aroma of a dish you're cooking, engaging your senses heightens your connection to the moment. Paradoxically, taking breaks can improve your ability to engage fully. Periodic pauses allow your mind to rest and recharge, preparing you to return with renewed focus.

Engaging fully in what you're doing is a powerful way to reclaim control over your attention and live a more intentional life. It is a skill that requires practice but yields extraordinary benefits. As you eliminate distractions, set clear intentions, and immerse yourself in the present moment, you will find yourself achieving greater productivity, creativity, and contentment. Begin today by focusing intensely on your next activity, and watch as the quality of your experience transforms.

7. The Truth of Impermanence

The Truth of Impermanence, also known as "Anicca" in Buddhism, is a fundamental concept reflecting the idea that all things are in a constant state of flux. This truth is one of the Three Marks of Existence in Buddhist philosophy, alongside suffering (Dukkha) and non-self (Anatta).

Everything in life is transient. Whether it's physical objects, emotions, relationships, or thoughts, all are subject to change and will eventually transform or come to an end. All living beings undergo cycles of birth, death, growth, and decay. Acknowledging these cycles helps in accepting life's natural progression. Understanding impermanence encourages non-attachment, which can alleviate suffering. When we realise that nothing lasts forever, we can enjoy the present moment without clinging or fear of loss.

Accepting impermanence can lead to spiritual growth. It provides insight into the nature of suffering and the path toward liberation and enlightenment. Emphasising the impermanence of sensations and experiences promotes mindfulness and awareness of the present moment. Recognising that everyone is subject to change fosters empathy and compassion for others. This understanding can improve relationships and encourage supportive behaviour. By embracing the Truth of Impermanence, you can cultivate a more resilient, mindful, and fulfilling approach to life.

Accepting impermanence doesn't mean you stop caring or striving. Instead, it allows you to live with greater ease, compassion, and appreciation for the ever-changing flow of life—everything is in a constant state of flux. From the seasons to relationships, careers, and even our bodies, nothing remains the same. Accepting this truth helps us let go of attachments and expectations. Clinging to things, people, or situations as if they will last forever often leads to pain when they inevitably change or come to an end.

8. Find Joy in the Simple Things

Finding joy in the simple things can significantly enhance your overall well-being and happiness. Here are some strategies to help you appreciate and find joy in everyday moments: Engage fully in the present moment. Whether you're eating a meal, taking a walk, or listening to music, focus on the experience and savour each aspect of it. Take time to appreciate what's around you. Slowing down allows you to notice and enjoy details you might otherwise overlook.

De-clutter your physical and mental space to focus on what truly matters. Reducing distractions can help you appreciate the simple pleasures life offers. German-born American painter Hans Hofmann has famously said, “The ability to simplify means to eliminate the unnecessary so that the necessary may speak.” Spend time outdoors and observe the beauty of nature. Watching a sunset, listening to birds, or taking a walk in a park can be incredibly uplifting.

Acknowledge and celebrate small achievements in your daily life. This could be completing a task or learning something new. Perform small acts of kindness for others. Helping someone or brightening their day can create a sense of joy and fulfilment. At the end of each day, reflect on the simple moments that brought you happiness. This reflection can help cultivate a positive outlook.

9. Summary

Life is full of uncertainties, and the present moment is often where the magic happens. Instead of fearing the unknown, approach it with curiosity and an open mind. Fulfilment in the now is not about achieving a perfect state of happiness but about embracing life as it is—messy, imperfect, and beautiful. By letting go of what you can’t control, you can find deep satisfaction in the present moment. Remember, the present is all you truly have—so make the most of it.

4

Going Beyond Avoidance

"Life is a mystery to be lived, not a problem to be solved."
—Søren Kierkegaard
Danish Philosopher (1813–1855)

1. Body as the Target of Mindfulness

Mindfulness, often misunderstood as a practice of seeking mental comfort or avoiding the physical realm, is far more profound and integrative than its surface interpretations suggest. It is a holistic approach to awareness that bridges the gap between mind and body, embracing both the conditioned responses and the natural rhythm of existence. This exploration will unravel the misconceptions surrounding mindfulness and shed light on its true purpose.

One widely held misunderstanding about mindfulness is that it involves turning away from the body and its conditioned responses, seeking refuge in the mind's comfort zone. This notion may stem from the idea that mindfulness is solely about achieving a state of tranquillity or detaching from uncomfortable sensations. However, true mindfulness does not advocate avoidance, but instead encourages a deep connection to the present moment, including the sensations and responses that arise within the body.

The body is an integral part of mindfulness practice. It serves as a vessel of awareness, a gateway to understanding the interplay between physical sensations and emotional states. By observing the body without judgment, practitioners can develop an intimate relationship with its conditioned responses—recognising patterns, accepting discomfort, and cultivating insight. This embodied awareness is a cornerstone of mindfulness, allowing individuals to confront rather than evade their inner experiences.

1.1 Body Scan Meditation

The body scan is a foundational mindfulness exercise that involves systematically bringing attention to different parts of the body. Practitioners observe sensations without judgment, developing a deeper awareness of their physical presence. This practice fosters a connection to the body and its conditioned responses, helping individuals identify and release tension.

1.2 Breath Awareness

Focusing on the breath is another core mindfulness technique. The breath serves as an anchor to the present moment, grounding practitioners. By observing the natural rhythm of the breath, individuals can cultivate a sense of calm and clarity, even amidst challenging emotions or sensations.

1.3 Mindful Movement

Mindful movement practices, such as yoga or walking meditation, emphasise the union of mind and body through intentional motion.

These practices encourage practitioners to notice the sensations of movement, fostering a sense of embodiment and presence.

2. The Art of Being Fully Present

At its core, mindfulness is the art of being fully present. It is an invitation to experience life in its entirety, from the ebb and flow of thoughts to the subtle shifts in physical sensations. Far from seeking mental comfort, mindfulness encourages practitioners to sit with discomfort, acknowledge it, and investigate it with curiosity. This approach fosters resilience and equanimity, qualities that arise when one learns to navigate life's challenges without turning away.

By embracing the present moment, mindfulness helps dismantle the illusion of separation between the mind and body. It urges individuals to understand that mental states are inherently linked to physical sensations and conditioned responses. For example, anxiety might manifest as a racing heart or tense muscles, while joy might bring a sense of lightness or warmth. Mindfulness helps to decode these connections, offering insight into the complex language of the body.

3. The Role of Conditioned Responses

Conditioned responses are automatic reactions shaped by past experiences and habitual patterns. They often arise in the body as fleeting sensations or reflexive behaviours, and they can dominate one's experience if left unchecked. According to a theory developed by Russian physiologist Ivan Pavlov, who won the Nobel Prize for Physiology or Medicine in 1904, through his experiments with dogs, he established how people associate two stimuli in their minds and react to one of them as though it were the other.

An Unconditioned Stimulus (US) naturally and automatically triggers a response without any prior learning. For example, food (US) naturally triggers salivation as an unconditioned response (UR). But when a Conditioned Stimulus (CS) is paired with the Unconditioned Stimulus, it eventually triggers a Conditioned Response (CR). He demonstrated how dogs salivated (CR) in response to the bell (CS) even when there was no food available.

This theory is widely used to significant effect. By gradually exposing patients to the feared stimulus (CS) in a safe environment, the conditioned fear response (CR) can be reduced or eliminated. Teachers can use positive reinforcement (US) to create conditioned responses (CR) in students, such as associating good grades (CS) with feelings of accomplishment and motivation. Advertisers use classical conditioning to create positive associations with their products. For example, a luxury car (CS) paired with images of success and wealth (US) can evoke feelings of desire (CR) in consumers.

Conditioned responses are a fundamental aspect of how we learn and adapt to our environment. By understanding how classical conditioning works, we can better understand human behaviour, treat psychological disorders, and even influence behaviour in positive ways. However, it's also important to be aware of how conditioned responses can lead to maladaptive behaviours, such as phobias or addictions, and work to address them through appropriate interventions.

Through mindfulness, practitioners learn to identify conditioned responses as they arise. This awareness provides an opportunity to pause, reflect, and respond intentionally rather than react impulsively. For instance, noticing tight shoulders during a stressful situation might prompt a mindful inquiry: "What am I feeling? Why is my body reacting this way?" This process transforms conditioned responses from unconscious habits into conscious moments of learning and growth. Indian-American author Deepak Chopra says, "Karma, memory, and desire are just the software of the soul. It's conditioning that the soul undergoes to create experience. And it's a cycle. In most people, the cycle is a conditioned response. They do the same things over and over again."

4. Mindful Inquiry

Mindful Inquiry is a practice that involves asking questions with an open, curious, and present mindset. It is rooted in mindfulness, a practice of being fully aware and engaged in the present moment without judgment. Mindful inquiry encourages deep listening, self-reflection, and a non-reactive exploration of thoughts, feelings, and experiences. There are four key aspects of mindful inquiry: presence, curiosity, non-judgmental openness, and compassion.

- Presence implies being fully present in the moment, allowing yourself to observe and experience without distraction.
- Curiosity is approaching questions with a genuine sense of curiosity, rather than seeking immediate answers or solutions.
- Non-judgmental openness is about observing thoughts, feelings, and experiences without labelling them as good or bad, right or wrong, and being open to whatever arises, even if it is uncomfortable or unfamiliar.
- Compassion is bringing a sense of kindness and compassion to the inquiry, both toward yourself and others.

For example, a self-inquiry might be, "What am I feeling right now, and where do I feel it in my body?" A relational inquiry, "How is this person's behaviour affecting me, and what might they be experiencing?" A situational inquiry, "What is this moment teaching me, and how can I respond with awareness?" Such mindful inquiries help you gain deeper insights into your thoughts, emotions, and behaviours, encourage a non-reactive approach to emotions, reduce impulsivity, and help you see situations more clearly, free from assumptions or biases.

5. The Integration of Mind and Body

The integration of mind and body is a holistic approach that recognises the profound interplay between mental and physical health. By fostering this connection through various practices and therapies, individuals can achieve greater overall well-being and resilience. Whether through ancient practices like yoga and meditation or modern approaches like health psychology and integrative medicine, these methods promote health and healing.

5.1 Philosophical Perspectives

French philosopher René Descartes said that the mind and body are distinct substances. He said living without thinking is like the life of a blind person. "To live without philosophising is in truth the same as keeping the eyes closed without attempting to open them." Monism, on the other hand, argues that the mind and body are aspects of the same substance. For example, materialism suggests that everything, including mental states, can be explained by physical processes. Holism views the mind and body as inseparable, emphasising the need to consider the whole person rather than isolating mental or physical aspects.

5.2 Psychological Perspectives

Psychosomatic medicine examines how psychological factors, such as stress and emotions, impact physical health and links conditions like hypertension, gastrointestinal disorders, and chronic pain to mental states. Cognitive Behavioural Therapy (CBT) is based on the idea that thoughts, feelings, and behaviours are interconnected. By changing negative thought patterns, individuals can improve both mental and physical well-being. Practices such as mindfulness meditation encourage awareness of the present moment, fostering a deeper connection between the mind and body.

5.3 Embodied Cognition

In their 1991 book *The Embodied Mind*, Francisco Varela, Evan Thompson, and Eleanor Rosch integrated insights from cognitive science, phenomenology, and Buddhist philosophy to argue that cognition is not confined to the brain but is deeply embedded in the body and its interactions with the environment. This emerging field in cognitive science suggests that mental processes are deeply rooted in the body's interactions with the environment. It challenges the traditional separation of mind and body, emphasising that physical experiences influence thinking. There are five key principles:

5.3.1 Body as Integral to Cognition

The body is not just a vessel for the brain; it actively shapes cognitive processes. For example, gestures, posture, and sensory-motor experiences influence how we think and perceive the world. All knowledge is grounded in sensory, perceptual, and motoric processes that are a function of the body's morphology and physiology.

5.3.2 Situatedness

Cognition occurs in the context of the environment. The mind is not isolated but interacts with the physical and social world. This means that cognitive processes are adapted to the specific situations in which they occur.

5.3.3 Action-Oriented

Cognition is not just about abstract thinking; it is fundamentally tied to action. We think to act, and our actions influence our thoughts. For example, the way we move through space affects how we perceive and remember locations.

5.3.4 Distributed Cognition

Cognitive processes are not confined to the brain but are distributed across the body, tools, and the environment. For instance, using a calculator or a map extends our cognitive abilities beyond our biological limits. The body acts as a tool for mental processing, distributing tasks between the brain and various bodily functions, much like a distributor. Examples include using gestures in communication and the impact of physical activity on mental well-being and learning.

5.3.5 Perception and Action are Intertwined

Perception is not a passive process but is actively shaped by our actions. For example, the way we move our eyes or hands affects what we see and feel. Seeing an action can activate the same motor plans that would be used to perform it, and vice versa, emphasising a functional coupling. We perceive the world in terms of our ability to interact with it. Our sensory information is often processed and filtered to guide our motor responses.

Words like "grasp" or "hold" are not just abstract concepts but are tied to physical actions and activate the same brain regions involved in the actual physical actions. Emotions are not just mental states but are experienced through bodily sensations. For example, feeling anxious might involve a racing heart or sweaty palms, which are physical responses. Remembering an event often involves re-experiencing the sensory and motor details of that event. For example, recalling a dance might involve mentally re-enacting the movements. Embodied cognition has influenced the design of robots that interact with their environment in more human-like ways, allowing them to learn and adapt through physical interaction.

6. Self-Realisation and Inner Growth

Taking life as a spiritual evolution is a profound perspective that invites us to see our existence as a journey of growth, self-discovery, and transcendence. This approach encourages us to move beyond the material and mundane aspects of life and focus on the deeper, more meaningful aspects of our being. Here are some key ideas and practices to consider when viewing life as a spiritual evolution:

6.1 Inner Work

Inner Work refers to the process of exploring and transforming one's inner world, including thoughts, emotions, beliefs, and subconscious patterns. It is a deeply personal and introspective practice that aims at fostering self-awareness, healing, and personal growth. This helps you recognise patterns that may be holding you back or guiding you forward. Engage in practices like meditation and journaling to explore your inner world and heal past wounds.

6.2 Connection to a Higher Purpose

Seek to understand your purpose in life. This could be through service to others, creative expression, or contributing to the greater good. A sense of purpose fuels spiritual growth. Align your actions with your values and higher principles. This creates a sense of harmony and integrity in your life. American philosopher Ralph Waldo Emerson writes, "The purpose of life is not to be happy. It is to be useful, to be honourable, to be compassionate, to have it make some difference that you have lived and lived well."

6.3 Embracing Change and Transformation

Accept that change is a natural part of life. Embrace transitions and challenges as opportunities for growth and transformation. Release attachments to outcomes, material possessions, and ego-driven desires. This allows you to flow with life and evolve spiritually. American writer Joseph Campbell says, "When we quit thinking primarily about ourselves and our self-preservation, we undergo a truly heroic transformation of consciousness."

Life has a higher purpose. According to Yogi-philosopher Sri Aurobindo, this purpose is to find and to serve the Divine. The Divine is not far, He is in ourselves, deep inside and above the feelings and the thoughts. With the Divine is peace, certitude, and even the solution of all difficulties.

7. The Life Divine

Sri Aurobindo's vision of a divine life on Earth, where matter, life, and mind are fully aligned with the divine reality, presents a hopeful and transformative perspective on humanity's future. He believed that individuals are capable of achieving higher states of consciousness and, through this process, contribute to the collective evolution of humanity towards a "Life Divine" on Earth. His philosophy invites individuals to engage in the process of self-transformation and to contribute to the collective evolution of consciousness. There are five key themes.

7.1 Evolution of Consciousness

The universe is not merely a material phenomenon but a manifestation of consciousness. Evolution is a process of spiritual unfolding, where consciousness evolves from matter to life, then to mind, and ultimately to higher states of awareness. The supramental consciousness is a state that transcends the mental plane, representing the next stage in human evolution. This supramental consciousness is characterised by unity, truth, and divine knowledge.

7.2 The Divine in All

All existence is a manifestation of the Divine or Brahman (the ultimate reality in Vedanta). The Divine is not separate from the world but is immanent in all things, including matter, life, and mind. The goal of human life is to realise this divine nature within oneself and to manifest it in the material world.

7.3 Integral Yoga

Aurobindo developed a spiritual practice called Integral Yoga, which aims to harmonise and integrate all aspects of the human being—physical, vital, mental, and spiritual. Unlike traditional forms of yoga that seek to transcend the world, Integral Yoga aims to transform the world by infusing it with divine consciousness.

7.4 The Transformation of Matter

Aurobindo envisions a future in which not only individual consciousness but also the material world itself will be transformed by the descent of the supramental consciousness. This transformation will lead to the creation of a divine life on Earth, where the physical, vital, and mental planes are fully aligned with the heavenly reality.

7.5 The Role of the Individual

Aurobindo emphasises the importance of the individual in the process of spiritual evolution. Each person has a unique role to play in the collective evolution of consciousness. By engaging in spiritual practice and self-transformation, individuals contribute to the larger process of global transformation.

8. Embracing the Unknown and Mystical

Embracing the unknown and mystical involves accepting uncertainty, finding wonder in the mysterious, and recognising the potential for growth and positive change within the unpredictable. It's about shifting from fear of the unknown to appreciating its potential for beauty and learning. Develop trust in the unknown and the mysteries of life. Spiritual evolution often involves stepping into the unknown and surrendering to a higher plan. Explore mystical experiences and teachings from various traditions. These can provide insights and deepen your spiritual understanding.

In *The Varieties of Religious Experience*, William James defines the standard features shared by all mystical experiences. He established four hallmarks.

8.1 Indescribable

Mystical experiences are partly ineffable in language. People who have supernatural experiences find it challenging, after returning to ordinary awareness, to adequately convey what happened to them during a mystical experience. No adequate report can therefore be given of such an experience. Mystical experiences are like emotions. People must experience it firsthand to truly understand it. Metaphors and poetic language can sometimes be used to convey the essence of a mystical experience.

8.2 Intellectual Quality

While mystical experience is perhaps ineffable like emotion, it nonetheless seems to experiencers to be a state of knowledge, understood as a perception of objective reality, whether it is or not. James refers to this characteristic as the "noetic quality" of mystical experience, providing genuine knowledge of "ultimate" realities which are unavailable to ordinary consciousness.

8.3 Transience

Mystical experiences typically last only a few hours, minutes, or even seconds. However, these experiences tend to deepen and become richer, persisting for more extended periods, with each subsequent experience a person undergoes. William James writes, "When the fruit is ripe, a touch will make it fall."

8.4 Passivity

Mystical experiences happen to people rather than people making them happen. Experiencers may undertake forms of spiritual preparation (for example, meditation) to become more open and receptive to mystical experiences. But people usually can't force a magical experience to occur simply by willing it. William James writes, "when the man neither care for nor desire anything but the eternal Good alone, and seek not himself nor his own things, but the honour of God only, he is made a partaker of all manner of joy, bliss, peace, rest, and consolation, and so the man is henceforth in the kingdom of heaven."

Ultimately, embracing the unknown and mystical is an act of courage — the willingness to walk barefoot through the mist of the unseen, guided not by certainty but by trust. In surrendering to the mystery, we move beyond the intellect into intuition, beyond fear into faith. The unknown is not an abyss but a vast field of possibility where the divine and the human meet. It is here that wisdom ripens, compassion deepens, and consciousness expands. When we learn to see uncertainty not as a void but as a sacred space of becoming, life itself transforms into a living meditation—a dance between the known and the infinite.

9. Summary

Viewing life as a spiritual evolution encourages you to move beyond the ego and connect with your true essence. The journey is unique for everyone, and there is no right or wrong way to evolve spiritually. As Chinese philosopher Lao Tzu said best, "Life is a series of natural and spontaneous changes. Don't resist them; that only creates sorrow. Let reality be reality. Let things flow naturally forward in whatever way they like." There is nothing to avoid in life; rather, it is about facing situations and responding. Trust your path and embrace the journey with an open heart and mind.

5

Self and Others

"His whole life has been torn between his desire to reveal himself and his desire to conceal himself. . . the discovery that we are irredeemably alone in certain respects, and know that within the territory of ourselves there can be only our footprints."

—R.D. Laing

Scottish psychiatrist(1927–1989)

1. Experiencing Situations

Distinguishing between "self" and "others" in a life situation involves a combination of self-awareness, perspective-taking, and emotional regulation. It is very common to find that different people experience the same problem in various ways. How one takes oneself and others around oneself plays a crucial role. Our emotions, thoughts, and bodily sensations are often unique to us and can help us recognise what is coming from within ourselves. Our values, beliefs, and priorities help differentiate our perspective from those of others.

Objectively assessing the situation by considering the facts, your role, and the roles of others is essential, but it seldom happens. Mostly, it is unclear where your perspective ends and another's begins. We often make assumptions about others' thoughts or feelings without considering their perspective. These assumptions can blur the line between self and others. It is essential not to confuse or absorb their emotions with your own. Practice recognising when you're feeling something on behalf of someone else versus when it's your own emotion - "Is this my reaction, or am I picking up on someone else's energy?"

1.1 Individualism

Individualism is a social and philosophical concept that emphasises the importance of an individual's rights, freedom, and independence over collective or societal concerns. The philosophy of Individualism embraces personal autonomy, self-expression, and the idea that individuals should have the freedom to pursue their own goals and interests without undue interference from external authorities or societal norms. According to American philosopher Ralph Waldo Emerson, "To be yourself in a world that is constantly trying to make you something else is the greatest accomplishment." Embrace your uniqueness — the world needs your spark. Celebrate your individuality — the world is your canvas. Irish author Oscar Wilde said, "Be yourself; everyone else is already taken."

1.2 Collectivism

Collectivism is a social, political, and economic philosophy that emphasises the importance of groups, communities, or society over individual interests. It advocates for the prioritisation of collective goals, co-operation, and social harmony, often promoting the idea that individuals are interconnected and that their well-being depends on the well-being of the community. German philosopher and political theorist Karl Marx said, "From each according to his ability, to each according to his needs." This principle encapsulates the idea of collectivism, emphasising communal sharing and mutual support.

Self and other orientations refer to the degree to which an individual's thoughts, feelings, and behaviours are directed towards themselves or others. Self-orientation emphasises personal goals, needs, and interests, while other-orientation focuses on the well-being of others, relationships, and group goals. These orientations are not mutually exclusive and can coexist or even be intertwined in various situations.

2. Boundary Setting

Learn to separate your emotions from those of others. For example, if someone is angry, you can acknowledge their anger without feeling it yourself. In the 1940s, Dr Fritz Perls, Laura Perls, and Paul Goodman developed a novel approach to study the individual's experience in the here and now, rather than delving extensively into past experiences. They encouraged the patient to focus on their current thoughts, feelings, and behaviours, with the idea that change can only occur in the present. By being fully aware of the present, individuals can make more authentic choices.

The concepts of Confluence, Introjections, and Retroflexions are often explored within the field of Gestalt therapy. These processes, while natural to human behaviour, can sometimes lead to inner turmoil and hinder personal growth. Understanding them is the first step toward overcoming their negative impact.

2.1 Confluence

Confluence refers to a lack of differentiation between oneself and others. In this state, individuals may blur the boundaries between their thoughts, feelings, and desires and those of the people around them. While some degree of confluence is essential for empathy and building relationships, excessive confluence can lead to a loss of self-identity and an inability to assert one's own needs and boundaries. One must learn to assert one's needs politely but firmly and dare to say "no" when necessary.

2.2 Introjections

Introjections occur when individuals internalise beliefs, values, or attitudes from external sources without critically examining whether these align with their authentic selves. This can result in feelings of discomfort or conflict, as the borrowed values may clash with one's true nature. It is essential to develop the habit of evaluating new ideas before accepting them as your own by seeking knowledge from diverse sources to ensure a balanced perspective.

2.3 Retroflexions

Retroflexions occur when individuals turn their emotions or impulses inward rather than expressing them outwardly. For example, instead of showing anger or frustration toward others, a person may direct these feelings toward themselves, leading to self-blame or self-sabotage. It is beneficial to find constructive ways to release emotions, such as through art, physical exercise, or open communication with trusted individuals.

Confluence, introjections, and retroflexions, while challenging, are not insurmountable obstacles. Embracing your authentic self and asserting your boundaries will pave the way for emotional balance and personal growth.

3. Personality as a Mask

The word "persona" in Latin means "mask." The personality we present to the world is not our true self. Still, it is a constructed identity that we use to navigate social interactions, conform to societal expectations, or protect our inner selves. Individuals wear a social mask or facade to present themselves to the world. It is the part of the personality that adapts to social norms, expectations, and roles. It serves a protective function, helping individuals fit into society and manage social interactions.

3.1 Social Conformity

In many social situations, people wear masks to conform to societal norms, avoid judgment, or gain acceptance. For example, someone might act more confident or agreeable than they truly feel to fit in.

3.2 Professional Roles

In the workplace, individuals often adopt professional personas that align with their job roles. This can involve suppressing certain emotions or behaviours to meet professional expectations.

3.3 Cultural Expectations

Different cultures have different expectations for behaviour, and individuals may wear masks to align with these cultural norms. For example, someone might suppress their true feelings to maintain harmony in a collectivist culture.

While masks can serve essential functions in helping individuals navigate social interactions and conform to societal expectations, there is a risk of losing touch with one's authentic self. By cultivating self-awareness, integrating hidden aspects of the self, and practising mindfulness, individuals can strike a balance between wearing masks when necessary and staying true to their inner selves.

4. Over-Identification with the Mask

One of the key dangers of wearing a mask is the potential loss of authenticity. When individuals become too identified with their personas, they may lose touch with their true selves, leading to feelings of emptiness, dissatisfaction, or existential crisis. Constantly wearing a mask, especially in professional or social settings, can lead to burnout, as the individual expends energy maintaining a facade that is not true to their inner self. Over-identification with the mask can create psychological conflict if the individual's true desires and emotions are repressed. This can lead to anxiety, depression, or other mental health issues.

Canadian-born American Sociologist Erving Goffman explained social interactions as a theatrical performance. In his dramaturgical model, individuals are likened to actors who wear masks to present themselves in various social contexts. Goffman distinguished between the front stage (where people perform their roles for an audience) and the backstage (where they can drop the mask and be themselves). Goffman also introduced the concept of impression management, where individuals consciously or unconsciously control the image they project to others, often by wearing a mask that aligns with social expectations.

People often present a curated version of themselves, masking their true nature to align with how they want to be perceived. French-born American writer Anais Nin writes, "We don't see things as they are, we see them as we are. And we don't see ourselves as we are, but as we wish to be seen."

Embracing the mask while staying authentic is a great life skill. By understanding when and why they wear masks, individuals can make conscious choices about when to adapt to social expectations and when to express their authentic selves. Awareness of the "masked" aspects of the self is fundamental. This involves acknowledging and accepting the parts of themselves that they may have repressed or denied as they navigate social roles and expectations.

5. Games People Play

Canadian-born American psychiatrist Eric Berne published a book, *Games People Play*, in 1964, examining social interactions as the "games" people engage in throughout life. These "games" are unconscious patterns of behaviour that people use to manipulate or control others, often to fulfil unmet psychological needs or to avoid intimacy. Berne also introduced the concept of life scripts, which are unconscious life plans that individuals develop in childhood. These scripts are based on early experiences and decisions, and they shape how people perceive themselves and their relationships. Berne said relatively straight on, "We are born princes, and the civilising process makes us frogs."

5.1 Transactional Analysis (TA)

Berne proposed that individuals operate from three ego states–Parent, Adult, and Child. The Parent ego state is influenced by internalised parental figures and involves behaviours, attitudes, and values that are learned from authority figures. It can be nurturing or critical. The Adult ego state is rational, logical, and objective. It processes information and makes decisions based on facts rather than emotions. The Child ego state is emotional, impulsive, and reflects the individual's inner child. It can be free and playful (Natural Child) or rebellious and defiant (Adapted Child).

Whenever two people interact, they operate from a specific Ego state. Now, if the Ego states of both participants match, their transaction is good. But if they are crossing, there is a problem. Understanding these transactions helps explain how people communicate and why conflicts arise. For example, if someone playfully asks, "How is the rain?" from a Child ego state and receives the answer "It is awful" from a Parent ego state, it is a bad transaction. But an answer like "feeling like dancing" from a Child ego state is a good one.

5.2 Games

Berne defines games as repetitive, predictable patterns of behaviour that have a hidden agenda. These games are often manipulative and serve to reinforce a person's psychological position or worldview. Every game has a payoff, which is the unconscious psychological benefit the person gains from playing the game. This payoff often involves reinforcing a negative belief about oneself or others, such as "I'm not good enough" or "People will always abandon me." Berne identifies several standard games, including: "Why Don't You, Yes But": In this game, one person presents a problem, and others offer solutions, but the person rejects every solution. The payoff is to prove that no one can help them.

In the "If It Weren't For You" game, one person blames another for their problems, avoiding responsibility for their own life. The payoff is to avoid taking risks or making changes. In the "Kick Me" game, a person behaves in a way that invites criticism or rejection, reinforcing their belief that they are unworthy of love or acceptance. In the "I'm Only Trying to Help You" game, a person offers unsolicited advice or help, often with the hidden agenda of feeling superior or in control.

5.3 Life Scripts

Berne introduces the concept of life scripts, which are unconscious life plans that individuals develop in childhood. These scripts are based on early experiences and decisions, and they shape how people perceive themselves and their relationships. Three standard life scripts are Winners, Non-Winners, and Losers. People with a "winner" script believe they will succeed in life and achieve their goals. People with a "non-winner" script may lead a mediocre life, avoiding both success and failure. People with a "loser" script believe they are destined to fail and may unconsciously sabotage their success.

By recognising and addressing these patterns, individuals can develop healthier, more fulfilling relationships and move towards greater psychological well-being.

6. I'm OK, You're OK

American psychiatrist and author Thomas Harris published a book in 1967 titled *I'm OK, You're OK*, introducing the concept of life positions, which are fundamental attitudes that people develop about themselves and others. He described four positions that are based on early childhood experiences and shape how individuals interact with the world.

6.1 I'm Not OK, You're OK

This is the position of the Child. People in this position feel inferior or inadequate compared to others. They may seek approval, feel victimised, or struggle with low self-esteem.

6.2 I'm Not OK, You're Not OK

This is the position of despair. People in this position feel that both themselves and others are fundamentally flawed. They may feel hopeless, depressed, or disconnected from others.

6.3 I'm OK, You're Not OK

This is the position of the Critical Parent. Individuals in this position often feel superior to others and may exhibit critical, controlling, or even abusive behaviour. They usually blame others for their problems.

6.4 I'm OK, You're OK

This is the healthy, adult position. Individuals in this position possess a balanced perspective on themselves and others. They feel worthy and capable, and they respect the worth and capabilities of others. Mutual respect, healthy relationships, and emotional well-being are key characteristics of this position.

Harris emphasises the importance of the Adult ego state in achieving the "I'm OK, You're OK" position. The Adult is rational, objective, and capable of making decisions based on facts rather than emotions or ingrained beliefs. By strengthening the Adult ego state, individuals can break free from the negative patterns of the Parent and Child ego states and move towards healthier, more balanced relationships. Harris has said, "Happiness is a choice that requires effort at times," to emphasise the importance of personal responsibility. That emotional well-being depends on conscious decisions and intentional actions.

7. Common Good Mindset

The common good mindset is a way of thinking that prioritises the well-being and collective benefit of society, rather than focusing solely on individual interests. It has deep roots in philosophy and ethics. In his book *Politics*, Greek philosopher Aristotle argued that the purpose of the state is to promote the common good, which he defined as the well-being of all citizens. English philosophers Jeremy Bentham and John Stuart Mill argued that actions should be judged based on their ability to maximise happiness or well-being for the greatest number of people.

Thinkers like John Locke in England, Jean-Jacques Rousseau in Geneva, and Immanuel Kant in Prussia emphasised the idea that individuals agree to give up some freedoms in exchange for the benefits of living in a society that protects the common good. They believed that the health, safety, and prosperity of the entire community are more important than individual gain. Making choices based on moral principles that consider the impact on others and the broader community.

8.1 I Am, Because You Are

Ubuntu, an African term meaning "humanity," embodies a philosophy that emphasises communalism, shared values, and interconnectedness within African societies. This concept is central to African thought, reflecting the idea that an individual's identity is inherently tied to their community and the relationships within it. The spirit of "A person is a person through other people" emphasises interconnectedness and the idea that one's humanity is realised through one's relationships with others.

8.2 Altruism

Altruism is the principle and practice of selfless concern for the well-being of others, often at one's own expense. It is a complex and multifaceted concept that plays a significant role in human behaviour and social interactions, usually seen as a cornerstone of moral and ethical systems. It involves acting out of a desire to help others without expecting anything in return, whether in the form of material rewards, recognition, or personal gain. The purest act of altruism is not expecting anything in return. In the Gita, it is referred to as Nishkama Karma.

Altruism is typically a voluntary act, not compelled by external forces or obligations. The primary goal is to enhance the well-being of others, whether it be individuals, groups, or society as a whole. Proponents of evolutionary theory suggest that altruism may have evolved because it promotes the survival of groups or species. For example, helping relatives (kin selection) or members of one's community can increase the chances of shared genes being passed on. Mahatma Gandhi said, "The best way to find yourself is to lose yourself in the service of others."

8.3 Compassion

Compassion is a profound awareness of another's suffering, accompanied by a desire to alleviate it. It involves both an emotional response (feeling empathy or concern for someone in distress) and a behavioural response (taking action to help). Compassion is often regarded as a crucial component of empathy, but it extends beyond merely understanding another person's pain—it encompasses a motivation to act and help.

Compassion provides comfort, reduces feelings of isolation, and helps people feel understood and supported. Practising compassion has been shown to improve mental and physical health, reduce stress, and increase feelings of happiness and fulfilment. Compassion fosters a sense of community, encourages co-operation, and can lead to more just and caring societies.

8. Summary

Living as part of society involves interacting with others, adhering to shared rules and customs, and contributing to the community's well-being. This includes respecting others, engaging in social activities, and understanding one's role and responsibilities within the societal structure. However, equally important is maintaining one's own unique identity and roles. Society provides a framework for individuals to develop and express themselves while also contributing to the collective.

Part II: Practices

As we stand at the threshold of a world increasingly shaped by artificial intelligence (AI), embracing ethical practices rooted in timeless values becomes vital to ensuring harmony, authenticity, and consciousness. By finding peace within, living spontaneously, accessing cosmic intelligence through meditation, and anchoring into timeless values, an adaptable, conscious framework is possible that emphasises transparency, accountability, empathy, and sustainability, thereby making the world more liveable.

6

Finding Inner Peace

"The two hardest tests on the spiritual road are the patience to wait for the right moment and the courage not to be disappointed with what we encounter."

—Paulo Coelho

Brazilian novelist (b. 1947)

1. Who Experiences?

Inner peace refers to a state of mental and emotional calmness, characterised by freedom from stress, anxiety, and turmoil. It involves a sense of harmony, contentment, and balance within oneself, regardless of external circumstances. Achieving inner peace often means being at ease with who you are, accepting life as it is, and finding a sense of purpose or fulfilment. Inner peace is not dependent on external circumstances but rather on one's internal state of mind and approach to life.

Antahkarana is derived from the Sanskrit words "Antah," meaning "inner" or "internal," and "Karana," meaning "instrument" or "organ." The Antahkarana is composed of four interrelated components, each playing a distinct role in the process of perception, cognition, and decision-making:

1.1 Manas is the mind or the thinking faculty. It is responsible for processing sensory input, emotions, and thoughts. Manas is often associated with the lower mind that deals with desires, doubts, and indecision. It handles sensory perception and emotional responses.

1.2 Buddhi is the intellect or the discriminating faculty. It represents the higher mind that enables discernment, judgment, and decision-making. It is the aspect of the mind that can distinguish between right and wrong, truth and illusion. Buddhi is responsible for reasoning, discrimination, and decision-making.

1.3 Chitta is the subconscious or the storehouse of memories and impressions. It is the repository of all past experiences, desires, and karma (actions). It is often associated with the emotional and memory-based aspects of the mind. Chitta stores past experiences and impressions, influencing present behaviour.

1.4 Ahamkara is the ego or the sense of individuality. It is the aspect of the mind that creates the sense of "I" or self-identity. It is responsible for the feeling of separateness and individuality. Ahamkara establishes the sense of self and personal identity.

By understanding and harmonising these components, one can achieve mental clarity, emotional balance, and ultimately, self-realisation. The goal is often to purify and transcend the

Antahkarana. Through meditation, self-inquiry, and other yogic practices, one seeks to go beyond the limitations of the mind (Manas), ego (Ahamkara), and the subconscious (Chitta) to realise the true Self (Atman), which is beyond the Antahkarana.

2. Store Consciousness

The concept of store consciousness, known as Alaya Vijnana in Sanskrit, is a key idea in the Yogachara Buddhist school, focusing on the nature of consciousness and the mind. Store consciousness is the foundational layer of the mind that stores all mental impressions, seeds of karma, and latent tendencies. It plays a crucial role in shaping our perceptions, thoughts, and actions. Store consciousness itself is neutral and non-discriminatory; it does not judge or categorise experiences but simply stores them as seeds.

Life often brings moments of pain and regret—those lingering echoes of past experiences remain as seeds, waiting to sprout when the right conditions arise. However, it is possible to "burn" these seeds. The most common and abundant are the feelings of hurt and regret.

Hurts and regrets often arise from situations where our expectations were unmet or where we feel we failed in some way. These emotions can build to an intense level, occupying our minds and holding us captive. Understanding their root causes is the first step toward freeing ourselves. Hurt may stem from betrayal, loss, or disappointment, while regret often emerges from actions we wish we had taken—or avoided.

Acknowledging the existence of these emotions is crucial. Attempting to suppress them can make them stronger, as unresolved feelings tend to surface repeatedly. Instead, approach them with curiosity and compassion, aiming to understand their impact on your life and mental well-being.

2.1 Cultivate Awareness

The path to healing begins with awareness. Take time to reflect on your emotions without judgment. Journaling can be a powerful tool to articulate what you are feeling and why. When you examine your feelings objectively, you may gain insights into their origins and lessen their grip. Practice mindfulness to stay present. Hurts and regrets often anchor us in the past or worry us about the future. Mindfulness techniques, such as meditation or deep breathing exercises, enable us to focus on the present moment, loosening the grip of past emotions.

2.2 Practice Forgiveness

Forgiveness is a liberating act, both for others and yourself. If someone has hurt you, forgiving them does not mean condoning their actions—it means choosing to release the hold they have on your emotional state. Visualise yourself cutting the cord that ties you to the hurt. Equally important is self-forgiveness. Many regrets stem from decisions we made or actions we took that we now wish were different. Remind yourself that you acted based on the knowledge and circumstances available to you at the time. Compassion toward yourself is the cornerstone of inner peace.

2.3 Accept What Cannot Be Changed

Acceptance is about embracing reality, even when it feels uncomfortable. Understand that the past is immutable, and regrets cannot rewrite what has already transpired. Rather than resisting these truths, lean into them and recognise that your experiences, both joyful and painful, have shaped the person you are today. Acceptance also means letting go of the belief that you could have controlled outcomes differently. Life is unpredictable, and circumstances often go beyond our control.

This transformative journey requires patience and persistence. It asks you to embrace self-awareness, forgive, accept, learn, surround yourself with positivity, and seek help when needed. With each step, the weight you carry lightens, and the path to inner peace becomes clearer.

3. Purifying the Mind

Purifying the mind is often likened to purging or cleansing negative impressions, mental residues, or unhelpful reactions that lead to suffering, unhelpful reactions, or distorted perceptions. These impressions, or "vasanas" in some traditions, can influence thoughts, emotions, and behaviours. By clearing these out, the mind becomes more transparent, more peaceful, and more receptive to positive qualities such as compassion, wisdom, and equanimity. Practices such as meditation, self-awareness, and ethical discipline are commonly employed to facilitate this purification process.

3.1 The Hindu Way

In the Hindu tradition, purifying the mind is done through self-discipline (Yama and Niyama). This involves following ethical guidelines such as non-violence (Ahimsa), truthfulness (Satya), purity (Shaucha), and contentment (Santosh), which help purify the mind by reducing negative tendencies. Regular meditation (Dhyana) cultivates mental clarity, concentration, and inner peace, helping to clear away impurities and disturbances. Repetition of sacred sounds or mantras (like Om or specific deity names) elevates consciousness and calms the mind. Cultivating love and devotion (Bhakti) through prayer, worship, and singing hymns shifts focus from ego to the divine, purifying the heart and mind. Developing detachment from worldly possessions and desires reduces mental agitation and promotes inner calmness. Acts of kindness, compassion, and selfless service (Seva) help remove ego and ill-will, leading to purification. Specific austerities, fasting, and cleansing rituals are sometimes observed to purify both body and mind.

3.2 The Buddhist Way

In Buddhism, purifying the mind involves cultivating positive mental qualities and eliminating negative mental states. Regular practice of meditation (Bhavana) helps calm the mind, develop mindfulness (Sati), and cultivate concentration (Samadhi). Techniques such as focused breathing, loving-kindness (Metta) meditation, and Vipassana are commonly practised. Cultivating sincere goodwill and compassion (Metta and Karuna) toward oneself and others dissolves ill-will, anger, and attachment. Developing an understanding of the true nature of reality—impermanence, suffering, and non-self—reduces misconceptions that lead to mental defilements. Following ethical guidelines (like non-lying, non-violent speech, and non-harming) supports mental clarity and purity. Contemplating the nature of change and the effects of actions encourages detachment from harmful desires and habits. Studying teachings such as the Four Noble Truths and the Eightfold Path helps discern the roots of mental impurities and the path to purification. Engaging in good deeds and charity fosters positive mental states and diminishes greed, hatred, and delusion.

3.3 The Stoic Way

In Stoicism, purifying the mind involves cultivating virtue and wisdom to achieve inner peace and resilience. The core practices focus on self-control, rationality, and aligning oneself with nature's reason (Logos). Regularly exercising control over desires and impulses helps diminish passions that disturb the mind, such as anger, envy, or greed. In practising Amor Fati, a Latin phrase meaning "love of fate" or "love of one's fate," everything that happens, including hardships, is accepted without resistance and mental agitation. Focusing only on what we can change helps free the mind from unnecessary worries and anxiety. Pre-meditation on challenges, called Premeditatio Malorum, a form of negative visualisation, prepares the mind to respond calmly and rationally. Striving to cultivate qualities like wisdom, justice, courage, and temperance cleanses the mind of vices and promotes tranquillity.

3.4 Purgatory

The Christian doctrine of Purgatory is a belief in a state or place of purification where souls who have died in God's grace but still require cleansing from the temporal effects of sin undergo a process of purification before entering Heaven. In a world where people often struggle with feelings of guilt, inadequacy, and imperfection, the idea of Purgatory offers hope. It suggests that even if one's life was not perfect, there is still a chance for purification and eventual union with God. This can be comforting for those who fear that their sins or shortcomings might prevent them from achieving salvation.

The concept of Purgatory as a place of healing and transformation resonates with modern psychological ideas about growth, healing, and self-improvement. Some see Purgatory as a metaphor for the soul's ongoing journey toward God, rather than a literal place of punishment, and as a personal transformation process.

4. The Science of Inner Peace

A substantial body of interdisciplinary research, combining insights from neuroscience, psychology, mindfulness, and spirituality, is available to help individuals cultivate inner peace in their lives.

4.1 Neuroscience of Inner Peace

The brain can rewire itself in response to experiences and practices. Mindfulness, meditation, and other peace-inducing activities can strengthen neural pathways associated with calmness and emotional regulation. The amygdala, a part of the brain responsible for the "fight or flight" response, can become less reactive through practices like meditation, leading to reduced stress and anxiety. The prefrontal cortex, responsible for decision-making and emotional regulation, becomes more active during mindfulness practices, helping individuals maintain a sense of inner peace even in challenging situations.

4.2 Psychological Aspects of Inner Peace

Mindfulness practices encourage individuals to stay present and accept their thoughts and feelings without judgment. This reduces rumination and promotes inner peace. Focusing on gratitude, compassion, and positive emotions can shift one's mindset toward peace and contentment. Techniques like cognitive behavioural therapy (CBT) and mindfulness-based stress reduction (MBSR) help individuals manage negative emotions and cultivate inner calm.

4.3 Physiological Benefits of Inner Peace

Practices such as meditation and deep breathing can enhance Heart Rate Variability (HRV), a measure of the body's ability to manage stress, resulting in increased emotional resilience. Chronic stress leads to elevated cortisol levels, which can disrupt inner peace. Mindfulness and relaxation techniques have been shown to lower cortisol levels. Inner peace is associated with a stronger immune system, as stress reduction improves overall health.

5. Mindfulness-Based Stress Reduction (MBSR)

Developed by American professor of medicine Jon Kabat-Zinn in 1979 at the University of Massachusetts Medical School, MBSR is designed to help individuals manage stress, pain, and illness through the practice of mindfulness, which involves paying attention to the present moment in a non-judgmental way. MBSR has been widely studied and is recognised for its effectiveness in reducing stress, anxiety, depression, and improving overall well-being.

MBSR is a mindfulness exercise. You are taught to focus on your breath, bodily sensations, thoughts, and emotions without judgment. This practice helps cultivate awareness and acceptance of the present moment. You systematically bring attention to different parts of the body, noticing sensations without trying to change them. This helps develop body awareness and relaxation. Simple yoga poses and stretches are incorporated to promote physical awareness, flexibility, and relaxation. The focus is on mindful movement rather than achieving specific postures. You are asked to pay attention to the sensations of walking and the connection between the body and the ground. This helps integrate mindfulness into daily activities, such as eating, washing dishes, or commuting.

6. Dopamine Detox

Dopamine is a neurotransmitter in the brain that plays a key role in the reward system. It is released when we engage in pleasurable activities, reinforcing behaviours that lead to rewards. However, in the contemporary world, many activities (such as scrolling through social media, binge-watching TV, or consuming sugary foods) can lead to dopamine overstimulation, which may reduce our ability to enjoy simpler, more meaningful activities and make it harder to focus on long-term goals.

The idea behind a Dopamine Detox is to take a break from activities that provide instant gratification, allowing the brain to reset its dopamine levels. By reducing distractions, you can focus more effectively on tasks that require sustained attention. When dopamine levels are reset, you may find more pleasure in activities that are less immediately rewarding but more meaningful in the long term. By breaking the cycle of constant stimulation, you can reduce your reliance on high-dopamine activities.

After a detox, you may find more pleasure in activities that you previously overlooked, like reading or spending time in nature. With less time spent on high-dopamine activities, you may have more time and energy to focus on meaningful goals. Reducing overstimulation can help reduce anxiety, stress, and feelings of overwhelm. Although it is not a scientifically validated practice, it is grounded in principles of neuroplasticity and dopamine regulation. By temporarily abstaining from activities that provide instant gratification, you can recalibrate your brain's sensitivity to natural rewards and develop a healthier relationship with technology and other high-dopamine activities.

7. Pratyahara

Pratyahara is the fifth limb of Ashtanga Yoga, as outlined by the sage Patanjali in the Yoga Sutras. It is often translated as "withdrawal of the senses" and refers to the practice of turning one's attention inward by disengaging from external stimuli. In everyday life, our senses are constantly bombarded with external stimuli, which can lead to distraction, restlessness, and a scattered mind. Pratyahara involves consciously withdrawing attention from these external inputs and redirecting it inward. This enables the mind to become calm and focused, thereby creating the optimal conditions for more profound meditation.

The mind, rather than its perception and action organs, is the object of focus when we intentionally turn inward and disengage from feeling. We stop physically and conceptually travelling through time and space. Similar to how regular light may be transformed into a laser by coordinating its different wavelengths, our energy gets more concentrated and focused when we engage with our senses, which are inherently divided, bifurcating, and dispersive. The Bhagavad Gita states, "Similarly to how a tortoise can steady its head by removing its limbs, so too can a man's wisdom become steady by removing his senses from sense objects."

As soon as awareness separates from the senses, it becomes susceptible. The awakening of the intuitive mind occurs when the senses are turned off. So, Pratyahara helps us break free from habitual thought patterns and mental patterns. When our minds are less divided, more open, and more complete, we are more likely to have the kind of creative insights that lead to novel solutions to problems, epiphanies, and outbursts of inspiration—insights that can absorb painful realities about oneself and remain steadfast through life's storms of cravings and provocations. Neither a natural talent nor a stroke of luck can account for such unwavering composure; it is a result of training.

8. Vipassana

Vipassana, meaning "to see things as they are," is a Buddhist meditation practice that focuses on self-observation and the purification of the mind. It involves cultivating mindfulness by observing sensations, thoughts, and emotions without judgment, ultimately leading to greater self-awareness and equanimity.

Vipassana emphasises observing the present moment, including physical sensations, thoughts, and emotions, as they arise and pass away. Practitioners are encouraged to observe without labelling, analysing, or getting carried away by experiences, simply noticing them as they are.

Vipassana recognises the deep connection between mental and physical states, highlighting how bodily sensations can influence thoughts and emotions. Through sustained practice, Vipassana aims to purify the mind of negativity and cultivate positive qualities, such as compassion and equanimity. By observing the impermanent nature of all phenomena, practitioners gain insight into the true nature of reality, leading to a deeper understanding of themselves and the world.

Through regular practice, we begin to realise that the essence of everything—including ourselves—is the ever-present ebb and flow of life. We come to terms with the fact that change is ongoing, uncontrollably and against our will. Over time, we come to see that clinging to transient and insubstantial things causes us pain. Our ability to remain objective and level-headed in the face of adversity is honed. After that, we start to feel the true meaning of happiness, which is not gratifying desires or preventing worries, but rather breaking free from that vicious cycle. When we finally calm down within, we can see how other people are hurting, and our wish is, "May they find what we have found: the way out of misery, the path of peace–metta-bhavana."

9. Summary

Living in peace is a gift you give to yourself—a gift of freedom, joy, and self-love. Your past does not define you; your choices in the present do. Choose to release what no longer serves you and step boldly into a brighter, more serene future. By purifying your consciousness and facing life as it unfolds without fear, you can break the cycle of suffering.

7

Living Spontaneously

"The nature of psychological compulsion is such that those who act under constraint remain under the impression that they are acting on their initiative. The victim of mind-manipulation does not know that he is a victim."

—Aldous Huxley
English writer (1894–1963)

1. Why Is Living Spontaneously Challenging?

Modern life is highly structured, with work, school, family obligations, and social commitments requiring planning and consistency. Spontaneity often clashes with these fixed schedules. Society usually values predictability and reliability, which can make spontaneous behaviour seem irresponsible or impractical. Many people are naturally risk-averse and prefer to plan to avoid potential adverse outcomes. They are fearful that their spontaneous actions may lead to mistakes or unintended consequences, and they avoid acting on impulse.

Constantly weighing options and overanalysing can make it hard to act spontaneously. People may second-guess themselves or feel paralysed by the need to make the "right" choice. The desire to have everything planned perfectly can stifle spontaneity, as it leaves little room for improvisation. Even leisure activities are planned or structured, reducing opportunities for spontaneous experiences. But above all, many people find comfort in routines and predictability, making it difficult to break out of familiar patterns.

Societies often encourage conformity to shared norms and values to maintain order and cohesion. From a young age, people are taught to follow rules, respect authority, and adhere to cultural expectations, which shape their behaviour and mindset. There are specific expectations regarding roles, behaviours, and success. These expectations condition individuals to pursue particular paths in life. Capitalist economies thrive on consumption, and people are conditioned to equate happiness and success with material possessions. Advertising and media play a significant role in shaping desires and creating a sense of inadequacy that drives consumer behaviour.

Social trends and fads, often amplified by social media, can condition people to adopt certain behaviours or interests to stay relevant or accepted. People are usually conditioned by their peer groups to conform to certain behaviours, styles, or attitudes to fit in. This can influence everything from fashion choices to career decisions. While this extensive interplay of social, cultural, economic, and technological forces provides structure and stability for the economic machine to run smoothly, it can also limit individuality and creativity.

2. Echo Chambers

The most potent feature of modern society is the echo chamber. It is a social phenomenon where individuals are exposed primarily to information, opinions, and beliefs that reinforce their existing views, while dissenting or alternative perspectives are excluded or minimised. This creates a self-reinforcing loop where people's beliefs become more entrenched, and they are less likely to encounter or consider opposing viewpoints. Echo chambers are particularly prevalent in the digital age, where algorithms and social media platforms play a significant role in shaping the information people see. Not only are we conditioned, but the conditioning is constantly renewed and deepened.

2.1 Key Characteristics of Echo Chambers

- Echo chambers amplify and confirm pre-existing beliefs, making it difficult for individuals to question or change their views.
- Alternative or opposing perspectives are often filtered out, either by the individual's choices or by algorithms.
- Echo chambers can lead to increased polarisation, as groups with differing views become more extreme in their positions and less willing to engage in constructive dialogue.
- People tend to seek out information that aligns with their beliefs and ignore or dismiss information that contradicts them, a cognitive bias known as confirmation bias.
- Within echo chambers, individuals often receive social validation from like-minded peers, which reinforces their beliefs and discourages dissent.

2.2 Causes of Echo Chambers

- Social media platforms and search engines use algorithms to personalise content based on users' past behaviour, preferences, and interactions. This can create a feedback loop where users are only shown content that aligns with their existing views.
- People naturally gravitate toward information sources and communities that align with their beliefs, avoiding those that challenge them.
- Platforms like Facebook, Twitter, and Instagram allow users to connect with like-minded individuals, creating insular communities where dissenting voices are rare.
- The rise of niche media outlets and online communities has made it easier for people to consume news and information that aligns with their worldview, rather than engaging with diverse perspectives.

2.3 Consequences of Echo Chambers

- Echo chambers have deepened societal divides by reinforcing extreme positions and reducing the likelihood of compromise or understanding between opposing groups.
- In echo chambers, false or misleading information can spread rapidly, as there is little exposure to fact-checking or alternative viewpoints.
- There is an alarming erosion of critical thinking. When individuals are only exposed to information that confirms their existing beliefs, they may become less likely to evaluate new information or consider alternative perspectives critically.

- Echo chambers can lead to the breakdown of shared social norms and values, as different groups become more isolated and less willing to engage with one another.

3. The Nature of Compulsions

In today's world, where external validation and societal pressures often dictate our actions, many individuals struggle with false identities—layers of personas formed in response to expectations—and the compulsions that stem from these constructs. Living spontaneously is about peeling back these layers to find your authentic self and embracing freedom in its purest form.

3.1 Understanding False Identities

False identities are the masks we wear to fit into social constructs, environments, or relationships. They often emerge from societal expectations, such as the pressure to conform to predefined roles like "the successful individual" or "the perfect parent," adopting traits or behaviours to avoid disapproval from others, developing coping mechanisms that manifest as identities different from our true selves, and striving to meet unrealistic standards, often at the expense of authenticity. These identities, while seemingly harmless, can disconnect you from your core values and inner desires.

3.2 Recognising Compulsions Tied to False Identities

Compulsions are repetitive behaviours or thought patterns that serve to reinforce false identities. Common compulsions include seeking perfection and validation through accomplishments, constantly prioritising others' needs over your own, protecting constructed personas at the expense of self-reflection, and overstructuring life to maintain control and avoid vulnerability. These compulsions often prevent spontaneity and hinder personal growth.

3.3 Steps to Clean Up False Identities

The journey toward authenticity begins with awareness and a commitment to self-discovery. Ask yourself probing questions, such as: "Who am I when no one is watching?" "What beliefs have I adopted from others that no longer serve me?" "What activities genuinely bring me joy?" Observe the moments when you feel compelled to act in a way that is out of alignment with your true self. What situations or relationships prompt you to adopt false identities? Identifying triggers helps you anticipate and address them.

4. Conquering Compulsions

Compulsions are repetitive behaviours or mental acts that a person feels driven to perform in response to an obsession or to reduce distress. These are often driven by anxiety or obsessive thoughts. The temporary relief they provide reinforces the behaviour, creating a vicious cycle.

4.1 Exposure and Response Prevention (ERP)

Exposure and Response Prevention (ERP) is a gold-standard therapy for compulsions. It involves gradually exposing yourself to the source of your anxiety (the obsession) while resisting the urge to perform the compulsive behaviour. Begin with less anxiety-provoking situations and gradually progress to more challenging ones. For example, if you feel compelled to wash your hands repeatedly, try touching a doorknob and then delaying washing your hands for a few minutes. Gradually increase the delay over time. The anxiety will decrease on its own without performing the compulsion.

4.2 Cognitive Behavioural Therapy (CBT)

Compulsions are often fuelled by irrational beliefs or fears (for example, "If I don't check the lock, something terrible will happen"). Ask yourself: "Is this thought based on facts or fears?" "What's the worst that could happen if I don't perform the compulsion?" "How likely is that worst-case scenario?" Replace irrational thoughts with more realistic ones. For example, "It's unlikely that something bad will happen if I don't check the lock." Accept that anxiety and discomfort are part of life. Instead of trying to eliminate them through compulsions, learn to tolerate them. This can reduce the power of the compulsion over time.

Conquering compulsions is a gradual process that requires patience, persistence, and often professional support. By understanding the underlying mechanisms of your compulsions and using evidence-based techniques like ERP and CBT, you can reduce their hold on your life and regain control. Remember, progress may be slow, but every step forward is a step toward freedom from compulsions.

5. Limiting Beliefs

Each person has deeply held convictions. Unfortunately, many such convictions are based on the notion that they are incapable, unworthy, or destined to fail. These beliefs stem from past experiences, societal conditioning, or negative self-talk, and they significantly hinder personal growth, success, and happiness.

5.1 What Are Limiting Beliefs?

Limiting beliefs are thoughts or assumptions that hold people back from achieving their full potential. They often manifest as self-doubt, fear, or a sense of inadequacy. Examples include: "I'm not smart enough to succeed," "I don't deserve to be happy," "I'll never be good at public speaking," "Money is hard to come by," or "I'm too old to start something new." These beliefs can impact various aspects of life, including career, relationships, health, and personal growth.

5.2 The Impact of Limiting Beliefs

Limiting beliefs prevent individuals from pursuing opportunities, taking risks, or reaching their full potential. People may unconsciously sabotage their own success because they don't believe they deserve it. Fear of failure or inadequacy can lead to procrastination and avoidance of important tasks. Limiting beliefs can erode self-confidence and self-worth, leading to feelings of inadequacy. Believing "I can't" or "I'm not good enough" can cause people to miss out on valuable experiences, relationships, or career advancements.

5.3 How to Overcome Limiting Beliefs

Self-reflection is the key to overcoming limiting beliefs. Take time to reflect on areas where you feel stuck or held back. Question the evidence: "Is this belief based on facts or assumptions?" For example, if you believe "I'm not good at public speaking," ask, "What evidence do I have to support this?" Replace limiting beliefs with empowering ones. For example, change "I'm not good at public speaking" to "I can improve my public speaking skills with practice." Look for examples that disprove your limiting belief. If you believe "I'm too old to start a new career," find stories of people who successfully changed careers later in life. Celebrate small victories and progress, even if they seem minor. This can help build confidence and reduce the power of limiting beliefs.

Limiting beliefs are deeply ingrained, but they are not immutable. With self-awareness, effort, and the right strategies, you can challenge and overcome these beliefs, unlocking your full potential and achieving greater success and fulfilment. Remember, the process takes time and patience, but every step forward is a step toward a more empowered and confident version of yourself.

6. Play Video Games

Playing video games has often been criticised for its potential adverse effects, such as addiction or reduced physical activity. However, research has shown that video games can also offer a range of cognitive, emotional, social, and even physical benefits when played in moderation.

6.1 Cognitive Benefits

- Many video games, especially strategy and puzzle games, require players to think critically and solve complex problems. Games like *Portal* or *The Legend of Zelda* encourage players to analyse situations, plan, and adapt to new challenges.
- Video games often require players to remember information, follow instructions, and pay attention to details.
- Action games, in particular, require quick reflexes and rapid decision-making. Players learn to process information and respond to stimuli more efficiently, which can translate to improved decision-making skills in real-life situations.

- Games that involve navigation, such as *Minecraft* or *Grand Theft Auto*, can enhance spatial reasoning and the ability to visualise and manipulate objects in three-dimensional space.

6.2 Emotional Benefits

- Video games can serve as a form of stress buster, allowing players to unwind and relax after a demanding day. Immersive games like *Stardew Valley* or *Animal Crossing* provide a calming, meditative experience.
- Games often present challenges and failures, teaching players to cope with setbacks and persevere. This can help build emotional resilience and a growth mindset.
- Playing video games can release dopamine, a neurotransmitter associated with pleasure and reward, which can improve mood and reduce feelings of anxiety or depression.

6.3 Social Benefits

- Multiplayer games like *Fortnite*, *Overwatch*, or *Among Us* require players to work together and communicate effectively. This can improve collaboration and leadership skills.
- For many, gaming is a way to build friendships and socialise, especially for those who may struggle with face-to-face interactions.
- Educational games like *Minecraft* or *Kerbal Space Program* can teach players about subjects such as science, maths, history, and engineering in an engaging and interactive way.

- Many games are available in multiple languages, and playing them can help improve language acquisition and vocabulary.

By integrating gaming into a healthy lifestyle, players can enjoy its many advantages while minimising potential downsides. Whether you're playing for fun, learning, or socialising, video games can be a valuable and enriching part of life. Jane McGonigal, a renowned game designer and author, is a strong advocate for the positive impact of games on real life. In her book, *Reality is Broken: Why Games Make Us Better and How They Can Change the World*, she argues that the principles of gaming can be applied to solve real-world problems and improve our lives.

7. Gamify Life

Jane McGonigal's idea of gamifying life involves applying the principles of games to make real-world tasks more engaging, rewarding, and meaningful. By setting clear goals, providing feedback, incorporating rewards, and fostering social connections, you can turn everyday activities into a game-like experience. Whether you're trying to build new habits, learn new skills, or achieve long-term goals, gamification can help you stay motivated and enjoy the process.

7.1 Key Principles

- Games help set clear goals and challenges. Games are engaging because they provide clear objectives and challenges. Applying this to real life can help you stay motivated and focused. Break down your goals into smaller, achievable tasks. For example, if you want to get fit, set a goal to complete a 30-day fitness challenge with daily milestones.

- In games, players receive instant feedback on their actions, which keeps them engaged and helps them improve. Use apps or tools that track your progress and provide feedback. For example, use a habit-tracking app to monitor your daily habits and see your streaks.
- Games often use progress bars, levels, and achievements to show players how far they've come. This sense of progress is highly motivating.
- However, most importantly, in games, failure is often an integral part of the learning process. Reframe failure as a chance to learn and grow. If you don't meet a goal, analyse what went wrong and try again with a new strategy.

7.2 Examples of Gamification in Real Life

- Turn household chores into a game where you earn points or rewards for completing tasks. You can even compete with family members to see who can do the most chores.
- Use a pedometer or fitness tracker to turn walking into a fun and engaging activity. Set daily step goals and compete with friends or co-workers to see who can get the most steps.
- Join a reading challenge where you earn points or badges for reading a certain number of books in a year. You can also compete with friends to see who can read the most.
- Gamify eco-friendly behaviours like recycling, conserving energy, or reducing waste. Use apps like *JouleBug* to track your green habits and earn rewards.

8. Practice Saying "Yes" and "No"

Say "yes" to opportunities that excite you, and "no" to those that drain your energy. This simple practice empowers you to embrace spontaneity while respecting your boundaries. Living spontaneously doesn't mean abandoning responsibility or structure. Instead, it's about making decisions based on intuition and authenticity, rather than external pressures, embracing uncertainty and allowing life to unfold naturally, finding joy in the unexpected and cherishing imperfection.

8.1 Simplify Your Life

Declutter both your physical and mental space. Let go of possessions, commitments, or habits that don't align with your values. Simplicity creates room for spontaneity. Italian genius Leonardo da Vinci famously said, "Simplicity is the ultimate sophistication." This quote tells us that stripping away the unnecessary and focusing on what truly matters can lead to a more refined, meaningful, and fulfilling life. Simplifying isn't about deprivation—it's about clarity, purpose, and elegance in how we live.

8.2 Cultivate Playfulness

Rediscover the joy of play—whether through art, music, sports, or exploring the natural world. Playfulness reconnects you with your inner child and encourages unstructured, creative expression. Irish playwright George Bernard Shaw said, "We don't stop playing because we grow old; we grow old because we stop playing." Playfulness is not just for children—it's a vital part of staying youthful, curious, and joyful throughout life. Embracing playfulness keeps our spirits alive and our minds open to new possibilities.

8.3 Follow Your Curiosity

Permit yourself to pursue interests without judgment. Curiosity leads to unexpected discoveries and deepens your connection to life. Legendary physicist Albert Einstein said, "The important thing is not to stop questioning. Curiosity has its own reason for existing." Curiosity is not just about finding answers—it's about the joy of exploring, questioning, and seeking to understand the world around us. Curiosity drives innovation, learning, and personal growth.

8.4 Celebrate Small Moments

Find beauty in everyday occurrences—a sunrise, laughter, or the aroma of coffee. Gratitude for the small joys cultivates a sense of wonder. American poet Maya Angelou said, "Life is not measured by the number of breaths we take, but by the moments that take our breath away," reminding us to cherish the extraordinary moments in life, big or small, and to find joy in the everyday experiences that make life truly meaningful. Celebrate the journey, not just the destination.

When we learn to live with intention yet move with ease, life becomes a graceful balance between purpose and play. Saying "yes" and "no" with awareness, simplifying what surrounds us, remaining curious, and cherishing small wonders—these are not isolated habits but a way of being that invites harmony between the inner and outer worlds. In embracing spontaneity, we rediscover the sacred rhythm of life—one that does not rush, grasp, or resist, but flows freely, guided by authenticity and joy. In this flow, every choice becomes a creation, every day a celebration, and every moment an unfolding miracle.

9. Summary

Cleaning up false identities and compulsions opens the door to profound transformation. The rewards include liberation from societal expectations and self-imposed constraints, a deep trust in your ability to navigate life authentically, experiencing happiness that stems from genuineness rather than external validation, and adapting to change and uncertainty with grace. Living spontaneously is not a destination but a continuous journey of self-exploration and growth. By shedding the weight of false identities and compulsions, you unlock the vibrant energy of your true self. Embrace this path with curiosity and courage, and you'll discover the boundless freedom that comes from living authentically. Live as if you are playing a game.

8

Accessing Cosmic Intelligence

"We carry within us all the wonders we seek around us."

Thomas Browne

English genius (1605–1682)

1. Breaking Free

The journey towards living authentically, guided by the innate wisdom of a clear mind and an open heart, begins with an act of liberation. Beyond emerging from internal compulsions—urges, cravings, and habits—it requires us to free ourselves from external influences such as cults, rigid schools of thought, and prescribed methods that may confine our natural intelligence and emotional clarity. By cultivating self-awareness, embracing inner peace, and fostering intellectual independence, we can reconnect with the boundless wisdom that resides within.

Intuition and wisdom are closely intertwined, but they aren't the same thing. Often described as a 'gut feeling' or a sense of knowing something without conscious reasoning, intuition is a rapid, subconscious process that draws on past experiences, patterns, and observations to provide insights. Wisdom is a profound understanding of life, people, and situations, accompanied by the capacity to make informed judgements and decisions. Wisdom is typically acquired through experience, reflection, and learning. In a two-way process, intuition adds to wisdom, and wisdom enhances intuition.

Intuition acts as a valuable signal, alerting us to important information or potential opportunities that our conscious mind might miss. Paying attention to our intuition and exploring its origins can lead to greater self-awareness and understanding, which are key components of wisdom. As we gain wisdom, our intuition often becomes more refined and accurate. A wise person has a broader perspective, a better understanding of cause and effect, and a greater ability to recognise patterns, all of which can enhance their intuitive abilities. It's essential to recognise that biases, fears, and incomplete information can impact intuition. Wisdom enables us to critically evaluate our intuitions, ensuring they are grounded in reality rather than based solely on assumptions or emotions. A clear mind and an open heart are established as prerequisites for relying on intuition.

1.1 The Clear Mind

A clear mind is achieved by decluttering mental noise and focusing on the present moment. It involves letting go of preconceived notions and judgements to embrace the infinite possibilities of now. American spiritual teacher Ram Dass (born Richard Alpert, 1931–2019) said, "The quieter you become, the more you can hear." Inner stillness allows for greater understanding and awareness. Like water, a mind is dynamic. In stormy conditions, visibility is impaired. When there is calm, clarity reigns.

1.2 The Open Heart

An open heart leads to compassion, connection, and authenticity. By fostering empathy and love, we can live harmoniously with ourselves and the world around us, tuning into the innate wisdom that stems from genuine human experiences. American author and disability rights advocate Helen Keller (1880–1968), who lost her sight and hearing after an illness at 19 months old, said, "The best and most beautiful things in the world cannot be seen or even touched - they must be felt with the heart."

Having an 'open heart and mind' implies being receptive, accepting, and willing to embrace new ideas, experiences, and perspectives. It's about approaching life with curiosity, empathy, and a lack of judgement. It's a powerful combination that can lead to greater personal growth, stronger relationships, and a more fulfilling life.

2. Recognising External Influences

Recognising external influences unconsciously controlling our lives is a crucial step towards greater autonomy and self-awareness. We consistently make confident choices, even when they don't align with our values or goals. There are patterns in our relationships, careers, spending habits, and free time activities. Certain situations or people consistently make us feel anxious, stressed, or unhappy. Examples of external influences include family expectations, social media, advertising, and cultural norms, even if they don't feel authentic.

2.1 Examine Your Beliefs and Values

Where did your beliefs about success, happiness, relationships, and the world come from? Be aware of the "shoulds" in your life—the things you feel obligated to do or be because of external expectations. Mahatma Gandhi emphasised the power of beliefs in shaping our lives, highlighting the need to choose them consciously: "Your beliefs become your thoughts, Your thoughts become your words, Your words become your actions, Your actions become your habits, Your habits become your values, Your values become your destiny."

2.2 Analyse Your Social Circle and Environment

Reflect on how your friends, family, and colleagues influence your decisions. Are you making decisions to fit in or gain approval? Are you being exposed to messages that promote unrealistic expectations or negative stereotypes? Pay attention to your thoughts, feelings, and sensations in the present moment without judgement. According to Eckhart Tolle, "We are not our feelings; we are not our thoughts. We are the awareness behind them." Creating distance from your thoughts and feelings so you can examine them more objectively is crucial.

By actively examining your thoughts, feelings, and behaviours, you can begin to identify the external influences that are unconsciously controlling your life and make more conscious choices that align with your actual values and goals.

3. Understanding Cult Dynamics

Cults often thrive on control, manipulation, and the suppression of individuality. They prey on the human desire for belonging and purpose, offering seemingly simple answers to life's complexities. Breaking free requires acknowledging their psychological tactics and remembering that actual growth stems from within, not from imposed doctrines.

3.1 Characteristics of Cults

Cults typically revolve around a single, charismatic leader who is seen as having special knowledge, abilities, or a divine connection. Members often develop intense devotion and obedience to this leader. Cults usually isolate members from their families, friends, and outside influences. This can be achieved through physical separation, control of information, or discouraging contact with non-members. Cults use various techniques to manipulate members' thoughts, feelings, and behaviours. By overwhelming recruits with affection and attention, they are induced into a trance-like state and their critical thinking is suppressed.

Cults create a sense of superiority and exclusivity, portraying themselves as the only true path or the chosen ones. Outsiders are often demonised or seen as enemies. Cults usually exploit members financially, emotionally, or sexually. Members may be required to donate their assets, work long hours for little or no pay, or engage in activities that violate their boundaries. Access to outside information is often restricted or filtered to prevent members from questioning the cult's doctrines. Members are threatened with punishment or expulsion if they disobey the leader or question the group's teachings.

3.2 Why People Join Cults

Cults often target individuals who are feeling lonely, isolated, or searching for a sense of community. Cults offer simple answers to complex questions about life, the universe, and everything. People who are going through a difficult time in their lives (e.g., loss of a loved one, job loss) may be more susceptible to cult recruitment. Some people are drawn to cults because they offer a vision of a better world or a utopian society. Learn to recognise the warning signs of cult involvement. Question everything and be wary of groups that discourage independent thought. Maintain strong relationships with family and friends who can provide support and perspective. If something feels wrong, don't ignore your intuition. American author Mark Twain, real name Samuel Langhorne Clemens (1835–1910) said, "Whenever you find yourself on the side of the majority, it is time to pause and reflect."

4. The Limits of Institutionalised Education

Institutionalised education, while a cornerstone of modern society, has inherent limitations that can hinder holistic learning and personal development. A one-size-fits-all style of education often follows a standardised curriculum, which may not cater to the unique learning styles, interests, or paces of individual students. This can lead to disengagement, especially for those who learn differently or have specific talents that aren't nurtured, which is a significant disadvantage no one bothers about. The system tends to prioritise uniformity over creativity, potentially stifling innovation and critical thinking.

Students are often assessed through standardised tests, which may not accurately reflect their actual abilities or potential. The focus on test scores and rankings overshadows the actual process of learning. Students prioritise memorisation for exams rather than deep understanding, leading to a superficial grasp of subjects. Many educational systems focus heavily on theoretical knowledge, which may not always translate to practical, real-world skills. This can leave students ill-prepared for the demands of the workforce or everyday life. Hands-on experiences, internships, and real-world problem-solving opportunities are often limited, which can hinder students' ability to apply their knowledge in practical contexts.

The competitive nature of institutional education, with its focus on grades and performance, can lead to significant stress, anxiety, and burnout among students. This can hurt their mental health and overall well-being. A coaching industry has emerged in India, focused on competitive exams. There is hardly any emotional or psychological support for students, leaving them to navigate challenges on their own.

While institutionalised education provides a structured framework for learning, its limitations highlight the need for reform and complementary approaches. Incorporating more personalised, experiential, and inclusive methods, along with a focus on holistic development, could help address these shortcomings and better prepare students for the complexities of the modern world. Alternative educational models, such as Montessori, homeschooling, or project-based learning, offer valuable insights into how education can be more flexible, student-centred, and relevant to real-life challenges. The apprenticeship method is also beneficial.

5. The Trap of Methods

Many pitfalls and limitations arise when we become overly reliant on specific methodologies, frameworks, or systems, whether in education, business, personal development, or other areas. While methods can provide structure and guidance, an overemphasis on them can lead to rigidity, stagnation, and a loss of creativity or adaptability. While methods can provide valuable guidance and structure, it's essential to recognise their limitations and avoid falling into the trap of over-reliance. By staying flexible, focusing on principles, and prioritising outcomes over adherence to a specific method, individuals and organisations can navigate complex challenges more effectively and foster a culture of innovation and adaptability.

6. Reconnect with Your Inner Self

Reconnecting with your inner self is a deeply personal and transformative process that involves tuning into your true feelings, desires, and values. In today's fast-paced, externally focused world, it's easy to lose touch with who you are.

Regular meditation can create a space for you to connect with your inner self. Nature has a calming effect on the mind, helping you feel more grounded. Whether it's a walk in the park, a hike in the mountains, or simply sitting by a river, spending time in nature can help you reconnect with your inner self. Activities like painting, writing, music, or dance can be a form of self-expression that helps you connect with your inner self. Creativity allows you to tap into your subconscious and express emotions that may be difficult to articulate. Allow yourself to play and experiment without worrying about the outcome. This can help you reconnect with your inner child and rediscover your natural curiosity and joy.

Reconnecting with your inner self requires self-compassion. Treat yourself with the same kindness and understanding that you would offer a close friend. Avoid judging yourself for your thoughts or feelings. Accept them as part of your experience and use them as a guide to understanding your inner self. Spending time alone can be a powerful way to reconnect with your inner self. It allows you to reflect on your thoughts and feelings without the influence of others.

Embrace silence as a way to tune into your inner voice. Whether it's through meditation, quiet walks, or simply sitting in stillness, silence can help you hear your inner thoughts more clearly. Prioritise self-care practices that nurture your body, such as regular exercise, a balanced diet, and sufficient sleep. A healthy body can support a healthy mind and spirit. This is a continuous process, and it's okay to seek support and guidance along the way.

7. Adopt Critical Thinking

Adopting critical thinking is essential for developing the ability to analyse, evaluate, and synthesise information in a logical and reasoned manner. It involves questioning assumptions, considering multiple perspectives, and making informed decisions. Ask questions that require more than a yes/no answer. Questions like "Why do you think that?" or "What evidence supports this?" encourage deeper thinking and exploration. Encourage questioning of underlying assumptions. For example, "What if the opposite were true?" or "What are we taking for granted here?"

7.1 The "5 Whys" technique

The Five Whys is a problem-solving technique used to explore the root cause of an issue by asking "Why?" five times. "Why" the problem occurs. Answer the question based on facts or observations. Repeat this process until the root cause is identified, typically after five iterations. For example, the machine stopped working.

- 1st Why: Why did the machine stop? Because it overheated.
- 2nd Why: Why did it overheat? Because the cooling fan failed.

- 3rd Why: Why did the cooling fan fail? Because the bearing was worn out.
- 4th Why: Why was the bearing worn out? Because it wasn't appropriately lubricated.
- 5th Why: Why wasn't it lubricated properly? Because scheduled maintenance was missed.

7.2 Socratic Questioning

Socratic Questioning is a disciplined method of asking thoughtful, open-ended questions to deepen understanding, challenge assumptions, and promote critical thinking. It encourages individuals to scrutinise their beliefs and reasoning. The questioning clarifies concepts ("What do you mean by...?"), probes assumptions ("What are you assuming...?"), questions evidence ("What evidence supports that?"), explores implications ("What might happen if...?"), considers alternative perspectives ("What is another way to look at this?"), and examines the reasoning ("How do you know that?"). Socratic questioning promotes a more profound understanding, encourages self-reflection, helps uncover underlying issues, and develops reasoning skills.

Fostering critical thinking is a continuous process that involves creating an environment where questioning, reflection, and analysis are encouraged. By implementing these strategies, individuals can develop the skills necessary to think critically, make informed decisions, and navigate complex situations with greater effectiveness. Whether in educational settings, the workplace, or personal life, critical thinking is a valuable skill that enhances problem-solving, decision-making, and overall intellectual growth.

8. Accessing Cosmic Intelligence

Accessing cosmic intelligence is a concept that involves tapping into a universal source of knowledge, wisdom, or consciousness that transcends individual human experience. This idea is often associated with spiritual, metaphysical, or esoteric traditions, and it can be approached through various practices that aim to expand awareness and connect with a higher or deeper level of understanding.

8.1 Ideal of Sthitaprajna

The concept of Sthitaprajna in the Bhagavad Gita refers to a person who has attained a state of cosmic intelligence characterised by steadfast wisdom and equanimity. This ideal is described in Chapter 2 (Verses 54-72) and Chapter 6 (Verses 7-32), where Lord Krishna explains the characteristics of a person who has achieved a balanced and tranquil mind, free from the disturbances of desire, fear, and anger.

The ideal of Sthitaprajna in the Bhagavad Gita represents a person who has achieved steadfast wisdom and equanimity in all aspects of life. Such a person is free from attachment, fear, and anger, and remains content and peaceful in all circumstances. The path to becoming a Sthitaprajna involves self-discipline, meditation, detachment, and devotion to the divine. By following the teachings of the Gita, one can cultivate these qualities and attain a state of inner peace and spiritual realisation. The Gita emphasises the practice of Karma Yoga (selfless action), Jnana Yoga (the path of knowledge), and Bhakti Yoga (the path of devotion) as means to attain the state of Sthitaprajna. "One must elevate oneself by one's mind, not degrade oneself. The mind is both the friend and the enemy of the self." (Gita 6.5).

8.2 Kundalini Yoga

Rooted in Tantra and Hatha Yoga traditions, Kundalini Yoga focuses on awakening the Kundalini energy, which is believed to lie dormant at the base of the spine. This practice combines physical postures (asanas), breath control (pranayama), chanting (mantras), meditation, and specific techniques to activate and raise this energy through the chakras (energy centres) to achieve higher states of consciousness and spiritual enlightenment.

There are seven chakras, starting with the Root Chakra, at the base of your body near the bottom of your spine and your pelvic area. This chakra helps keep you grounded. The second, Sacral Chakra, located between your belly button and your pubic bone, is associated with sexual fulfilment, emotional intelligence, and social acceptance. The Solar Plexus Chakra is situated between the upper abdomen and the chest bone and is related to the liver, gallbladder, stomach, spleen, and pancreas. It is thought to be your source of individual power or your gut instinct. Your fourth chakra is located in the chest, supporting blood circulation and the function of the vagus nerve. The Throat Chakra is associated with personal expression, self-awareness, and discovering the truth. The Third-Eye Chakra is located on your brow. It governs rational thoughts, insights, and intuition. These six chakras are within the body. The seventh one is located proximal to the top of the head, known as the Crown Chakra, which serves as the bridge between your physical body and the spiritual world.

Kundalini is often depicted as a coiled serpent, representing its potential energy and the dormant state in which it resides in the Root Chakra. Kundalini can be awakened and activated to rise through the Sushumna Nadi (central energy channel in the spine). As Kundalini ascends, it is believed to pass through the other six chakras, potentially bringing about profound spiritual and physical transformations. The ultimate goal of Kundalini's journey is to reach the Crown Chakra at the top of the head, symbolising enlightenment and union with the divine, as well as access to cosmic intelligence.

8.3 Individuation Method

The Individuation Process is the central concept in Carl Jung's analytical psychology, referring to the journey of self-realisation and psychological integration that leads an individual to become their true self. Jung believed that the goal of life is to achieve wholeness by integrating the conscious and unconscious aspects of the psyche. This process involves confronting and reconciling the various parts of the self, including the ego, the shadow, the anima/animus, and the Self.

The Self is the central archetype in Jung's theory, representing the totality of the psyche, encompassing both the conscious and unconscious aspects. The ego is the conscious part of the psyche that mediates between the inner world (the unconscious) and the outer world (reality). The shadow consists of the unconscious aspects of the personality that the ego has rejected or repressed. The anima (in men) and animus (in women) are the archetypal representations of the feminine and masculine aspects of the psyche, respectively. They serve as bridges between the conscious and unconscious mind.

The first step in individuation is to differentiate the persona from the true self. The next step is to confront and integrate the shadow. This involves acknowledging the dark, unconscious aspects of the psyche that we have repressed or denied. After integrating the shadow, the individual must confront and integrate the anima or animus. This involves recognising and embracing the qualities of the opposite gender within oneself. Integrating the anima/animus leads to greater psychological balance and creativity. The final stage of individuation is the encounter with the Self. This involves recognising the Self as the true centre of the psyche and integrating it into conscious awareness.

Accessing cosmic intelligence is a profoundly personal and multifaceted journey that can involve a combination of spiritual, mental, and physical practices. Whether through meditation, nature immersion, creative expression, or scientific inquiry, the goal is to expand your awareness and connect with a deeper, universal source of wisdom. Remember that this is a process of exploration and discovery; it's essential to approach it with an open mind and heart.

When we attune ourselves to cosmic intelligence, we move beyond the limits of personal intellect and enter a realm where intuition, synchronicity, and insight flow effortlessly. This is the state where the universe seems to whisper answers, not through logic but through resonance. It is a communion rather than a conquest — an awakening to the truth that we are not separate from the cosmos but expressions of its boundless creativity. By quieting the noise of the mind and opening the heart, we align with this infinite field of consciousness, allowing wisdom to emerge not as information, but as illumination.

9. Summary

Choosing to live by the innate wisdom of a clear mind and an open heart is a profoundly courageous act. It is the decision to step away from prescribed paths and embrace the boundless potential of your inner self. Through self-awareness, critical thinking, and emotional clarity, you can create a life led by authenticity, freedom, and love, becoming a beacon of inspiration for others seeking their liberation.

9
Twenty Timeless Values

A system of morality which is based on relative emotional values is a mere illusion, a thoroughly vulgar conception which has nothing sound in it and nothing true.

Socrates
Greek philosopher (470–399 BCE)

1. Ethical Behaviour

Ethical behaviour is a cornerstone of a just and harmonious society. It involves making choices that reflect moral principles and considering the impact of those choices on others. Whether in personal life, business, or leadership, ethical behaviour builds trust, fosters positive relationships, and contributes to the greater good. By understanding and practising ethical behaviour, individuals and organisations can create a more ethical and sustainable world.

Trust and reputation are two interrelated concepts that play a crucial role in personal relationships, business, and society. People invest a great deal of energy in building trust and reputation, as it reaps them significant benefits and preference in high-stakes competition. Trust is the foundation of all meaningful relationships, while reputation shapes how others perceive and interact with you. Together, they create a virtuous cycle of credibility, loyalty, and ethical behaviour.

1.1 Trust

Trust is the confidence or belief in the reliability, integrity, and honesty of a person, organisation, or system. It involves a willingness to be vulnerable based on the expectation that the other party will act predictably and ethically. Trust enables individuals and organisations to work together effectively. It reduces the need for constant oversight and control, making collaboration smoother. When trust exists, misunderstandings and conflicts are less likely to escalate. People are more willing to resolve issues amicably. In business, trust proves the confidence that the other party will adhere to moral and ethical principles and the belief that the other party can fulfil their commitments or responsibilities. Trust helps partners navigate disagreements without damaging the relationship. Trust is the foundation of all healthy relationships, whether personal or professional. American author Stephen R. Covey (1932–2012) in *The 7 Habits of Highly Effective People* writes, "Trust is the glue of life. It's the most essential ingredient in effective communication. It's the foundational principle that holds all relationships."

1.2 Reputation

Reputation is the collective perception or opinion that others hold about an individual, organisation, or brand based on past actions, behaviour, and performance. Reputation rests on the alignment between actions and stated values, how others perceive and discuss the entity, and the extent to which the entity is seen as trustworthy in taking responsibility for its actions and outcomes. Reputation is often built over time but can be damaged quickly. In his play *Othello*, William Shakespeare writes for his character Iago, "Reputation, reputation, reputation! O, I have lost my reputation! I have lost the immortal part of myself, and what remains is bestial." This highlights the immense value placed on reputation and the devastating impact its loss can have on an individual. Shakespeare's Iago laments the loss of reputation as the loss of one's essence, suggesting that it is a core part of one's identity and worth.

Timeless human values are principles and ideals that have been cherished across cultures, generations, and historical periods. These values often serve as the foundation for ethical behaviour, personal growth, and societal harmony. While the specific expression of these values may vary, their essence remains universal.

2. The Sources of Human Values

Values are diverse and multifaceted, often rooted in a combination of cultural, philosophical, religious, and personal influences.

2.1 Religion and Spirituality

Many of the world's major religions—such as Hinduism, Buddhism, Judaism, Christianity, Islam, and others—provide moral frameworks and ethical guidelines that shape human values. These traditions often emphasise virtues like compassion, honesty, humility, and justice.

2.2 Philosophical Traditions

Both Eastern and Western philosophical systems have explored the nature of morality, ethics, and human values. Thinkers such as Aristotle, Confucius, Kant, and Nietzsche have significantly contributed to our understanding of virtues, duty, and the concept of the good life. Aristotle's concept of *eudaimonia* (flourishing) or Confucius's emphasis on *ren* (benevolence) are examples of these great values.

2.3 Cultural Traditions

Every culture has its own set of values that are passed down through generations via stories, rituals, customs, and social norms. These values are often deeply embedded in the collective identity of a community. The value of *Ubuntu* in African cultures, which emphasises community and interconnectedness, is similar to the Japanese concept of *wa* (harmony).

2.4 Artwork

Stories, myths, and artistic expressions often convey moral lessons and explore human values. Literature, film, theatre, and other forms of art can inspire and challenge people to reflect on their values. Russian writer Leo Tolstoy valued honesty and moral integrity above all else. He believed that individuals should live by their conscience and seek truth in all aspects of life. French writer Victor Hugo was a fierce advocate for social justice and equality. He believed in the inherent dignity of all human beings, regardless of their social status, and often highlighted the plight of the poor and marginalised in his works.

Scientific inquiry and rational thought can also inform human values, particularly in areas like truth-seeking, intellectual honesty, and the pursuit of knowledge. The scientific method promotes values like scepticism, evidence-based reasoning, and open-mindedness. Peer groups, workplaces, and social organisations can influence what people consider essential. Economic ideologies and practices can influence values related to work, wealth, and fairness.

3. Timeless Values

Human values are not static; they evolve as societies change and new challenges arise. So, what is the idea behind timeless values? These are the values that transcend time, geography, and individual circumstances, offering a universal framework for ethical behaviour, personal growth, and societal harmony. The idea is that while societies and technologies evolve, specific core values remain constant because they address fundamental aspects of human nature and the human condition. There are five key aspects: universality, moral and ethical foundation, resilience across time, focus on human dignity and well-being, and adaptability.

Timeless values are not confined to a specific culture, religion, or historical period. Timeless values serve as a moral compass, guiding individuals in making ethical decisions, even in complex or rapidly changing circumstances. These values have endured throughout history because they address fundamental human needs and aspirations. They remain relevant even as societies evolve technologically, politically, and socially. The inherent worth of every individual is celebrated. Most importantly, these are not static or archaic. While timeless values themselves remain constant, their application can adapt to different contexts. This adaptability helps timeless values stay relevant in a changing world.

4. The List of Twenty Timeless Values

4.1 Compassion and Empathy

The ability to understand and share the feelings of others, and to act with kindness and care. Compassion drives people to help those in need and fosters a sense of interconnectedness. English historian Arnold Toynbee (1852–1883) writes, "Compassion is the desire that moves the individual self to widen the scope of its self-concern to embrace the whole of the universal self." On a lighter note, empathy is like a good pair of shoes—it helps you walk a mile in someone else's feet without getting blisters!

4.2 Honesty and Integrity

Being truthful and acting with moral uprightness. Honesty builds trust, while integrity ensures that one's actions align with their values, even when no one is watching. American religious leader James E. Faust (1920–2007) writes, "Honesty is more than not lying. It is truth-telling, truth-speaking, truth-living, and truth-loving." Honesty and integrity are essential for the smooth functioning of society, even when they are not always in the spotlight. It is like a good Wi-Fi signal—you don't notice it until it's gone, and then everything falls apart!

4.3 Respect

Valuing the dignity and worth of every individual, regardless of differences. Respect fosters tolerance, inclusivity, and peaceful coexistence. Irish novelist Laurence Sterne (1713–1768) writes, "Respect for ourselves guides our morals, respect for others guides our manners." How we treat others often reflects how we're treated in return. It is like a boomerang—throw it out, and it'll come right back to you (unless you're terrible at throwing)!

4.4 Justice and Fairness

The pursuit of equality and the fair treatment of all people. Justice ensures that individuals are treated equitably and that wrongdoing is addressed. American civil rights activist Martin Luther King

Jr. (1929–1968) said, "Injustice anywhere is a threat to justice everywhere." Injustice, wherever it occurs, can erode the very foundation of fairness and equality for all. It is like a well-balanced scale—if you tip it too far in one direction, someone's bound to get weighed down!

4.5 Courage

The strength to face fear, adversity, or uncertainty. Courage empowers individuals to stand up for what is right, even in the face of opposition or peril. Beatnik Ambrose Redmoon, real name James Neil Hollingworth (1933–1996), said, "Courage is not the absence of fear, but rather the judgment that something else is more important than fear." Courage is like a muscle—it doesn't show up until you're brave enough to flex it! Courage often reveals itself in moments when we step out of our comfort zone and act.

4.6 Gratitude

Acknowledging and appreciating the good in one's life. Gratitude fosters contentment, humility, and a positive outlook. American author Melody Beattie (1948–2025) writes, "Gratitude turns what we have into enough, and more. It turns denial into acceptance, chaos into order, and confusion into clarity. It can turn a meal into a feast, a house into a home, a stranger into a friend." Gratitude can transform our perspective, helping us appreciate the abundance in our lives and find joy in the simplest things. Gratitude is like a magic eraser—it doesn't change the past, but it sure makes the present look a lot brighter!

4.7 Humility

Recognising one's limitations and valuing the contributions of others. Humility encourages continuous learning and prevents arrogance. According to American pastor Ralph W. Sockman (1889–1970), "True humility is intelligent self-respect which keeps us from thinking too highly or too meanly of ourselves. It makes us modest by reminding us how far we have come short of what we can be." Subtlety and self-awareness are hallmarks of humility. It's like a good joke—it's best delivered without pointing out how funny it is.

4.8 Love

A deep sense of care and connection, whether for family, friends, or humanity as a whole. Love is a driving force for selflessness, sacrifice, and unity. Ancient Chinese philosopher Lao Tzu said, "Being deeply loved by someone gives you strength, while loving someone deeply gives you courage." Love thrives on closeness but can endure even when apart. Like a Wi-Fi connection—it's strongest when you're close, but it can still work from a distance if you've got a good signal!

4.9 Wisdom

The ability to make sound judgements and decisions based on knowledge, experience, and understanding. Wisdom guides individuals to act in ways that benefit both themselves and others. Wisdom is gained through continuous learning and experience, rather than relying solely on formal education. Albert Einstein said, "Wisdom is not a product of schooling but of the lifelong attempt to acquire it." Wisdom is like a good GPS—it doesn't just tell you where to go, it also warns you about the traffic jams ahead! It not only guides us but also helps us navigate life's challenges with foresight.

4.10 Responsibility

Being accountable for one's actions and their consequences. Responsibility encourages individuals to make positive contributions to their communities and the world. Abraham Lincoln said, "You cannot escape the responsibility of tomorrow by evading it today." In the film *Spider-Man*, the character Uncle Ben says, "With great power comes great responsibility." Responsibility is tied to the influence and abilities we possess, urging us to use them wisely and for the greater good.

4.11 Forgiveness

Letting go of resentment and the desire for revenge. Forgiveness promotes healing, reconciliation, and personal growth. There is an anonymous quote, "Forgiveness is not about forgetting. It is about letting go of the hurt and finding peace within yourself. It is a gift you give to yourself, freeing your heart from the weight of resentment. In a tit-for-tat world of today, forgiveness is the best revenge—it leaves the other person wondering why you're not mad anymore!

4.12 Generosity

The willingness to give time, resources, or support to others without expecting anything in return. Generosity fosters a sense of abundance and a strong sense of community. Generosity has a way of enriching both the giver and the receiver. There is an anonymous quote, "Generosity is not just about giving material things; it's about giving your time, your attention, your love, and your kindness. The more you give, the richer your life becomes." Generosity is best understood as the art of giving without expecting a return, except maybe a smile or a warm, fuzzy feeling!

4.13 Perseverance

The determination to keep going despite challenges or setbacks. Perseverance is essential for achieving long-term goals and overcoming obstacles. Perseverance is about staying committed to your goals, no matter the obstacles. Scottish politician Walter Elliot (1888–1958) said, "Perseverance is not a long race; it is many short races one after the other. Keep moving forward, even when the path is tough, and you'll eventually reach your destination." When you're tired of climbing the mountain, remember—you're halfway to the top!

4.14 Peace

The pursuit of harmony, both within oneself and in relationships with others. Peace is a cornerstone of a stable and thriving society. True peace often begins within and spreads outward to the world around us. As says one anonymous axiom, "Peace is not the absence of conflict, but the ability to handle it with a calm heart and a clear mind. It begins within you and radiates outward." When the world is loud, it's the quiet in your soul that keeps you sane!

4.15 Freedom

The ability to think, speak, and act according to one's own will, within the bounds of respect for others. Freedom is essential for personal autonomy and self-expression. True freedom lies in the ability to live authentically and make choices that align with your most deeply held values. According to Brazilian author Paulo Coelho, "Freedom is not the absence of commitments, but the ability to choose—and commit myself to—what is best for my soul."

4.16 Unity

The recognition that, despite differences, humanity is interconnected. Unity promotes cooperation, collaboration, and collective well-being. Unity brings people together, creating a powerful force for positive change and shared success. American author Matthew J. T. "Mattie" Stepanek (1990–2004) writes, "Unity is strength. When teamwork and collaboration are present, wonderful things can be achieved. Together, we can move mountains." When we stand together, even the smallest steps can lead to giant leaps!

4.17 Curiosity and Learning

The desire to explore, understand, and grow. Curiosity drives innovation, personal development, and the advancement of knowledge. Curiosity fuels the desire to learn, grow, and explore the endless possibilities of knowledge. According to Albert Einstein, "The important thing is not to stop questioning. Curiosity has its own reason for existing. Never lose a holy curiosity." Curiosity didn't just kill the cat—it made it the most intelligent cat in the room!

4.18 Patience

The ability to wait calmly and endure difficulties without frustration. Patience allows for thoughtful decision-making and long-term planning. Patience is a virtue that enables us to navigate life's challenges with grace and resilience. American author and speaker Joyce Meyer says, "Patience is not the ability to wait, but the ability to keep a good attitude while waiting." When life gives you lemons, take your time to make the best lemonade—no rush!

4.19 Simplicity

Valuing what is essential and avoiding excess. Simplicity encourages mindfulness, contentment, and sustainability. Simplicity often brings clarity and focus, allowing us to appreciate the essence of things. Leonardo da Vinci said, "Simplicity is the ultimate sophistication. It is about subtracting the obvious and adding the meaningful." Why complicate life when you can just hit the 'easy' button?

4.20 Hope

The belief in the possibility of a better future. Hope inspires resilience, optimism, and the pursuit of positive change. Hope is a resilient force that keeps us moving forward, even in the darkest of times. American poetess Emily Dickinson (1830–1886) writes, "Hope is the thing with feathers that perches in the soul—and sings the tunes without the words—and never stops at all." When life gives you clouds, it's just a reminder that the sun is still up there somewhere!

These timeless values have shaped human history and continue to guide individuals and societies toward a more ethical, compassionate, and fulfilling existence—no wonder they are quoted and cited by people worldwide across different periods. While the world evolves, these principles remain a compass for navigating life's challenges and opportunities.

5. Having a Personal Value Code

A value code serves as a moral compass, helping you make decisions that align with your beliefs and principles, even in challenging situations. It enables you to prioritise what truly matters to you, reducing confusion and allowing you to focus on what's essential in life. Living by a set of values fosters consistency between your actions and beliefs, which builds trust and respect from others. When you live in alignment with your values, you feel more authentic and confident in yourself.

During tough times, your values code can provide a sense of stability and purpose, helping you stay grounded and motivated. A value code challenges you to continually reflect on and improve yourself, fostering personal development. When you know your values, you can build deeper, more meaningful connections with people who share or respect those values. In essence, a personal value code serves as the foundation for a purposeful, authentic, and fulfilling life. It's not just about knowing what you stand for—it's about living it.

6. Summary

Values are the map that guides you through life's journey, helping you navigate challenges, make meaningful choices, and stay true to yourself. Without values, it's hard to know what you're striving for or what truly matters to you. Life can feel aimless. Decisions may become reactive or based on external pressures rather than your core beliefs, leading to regret or confusion. Living without values is like wandering without a map—directionless, uncertain, and prone to getting lost.

10

Framework of Neo-ethical Living

"Morality doesn't mean 'following divine commands'. It means 'reducing suffering'. Hence, in order to act morally, you don't need to believe in any myth or story. You just need to develop a deep appreciation of suffering."

—Yuval Noah Harari
Israeli Author (b. 1976)

1. An Approach to Harmonious and Sustainable Living

Neo-ethical living represents a modern reinterpretation of ethics, designed to create harmony between individuals, societies, and the planet they inhabit. It emphasises interconnectedness, adaptability, and sustainability in the face of contemporary challenges such as environmental degradation, technological innovation, and social inequity. This concluding chapter provides a framework for Neo-ethical Living, integrating philosophical principles, practical guidelines, and a vision for a better future. This holistic approach seeks to balance human needs with the planet's ecological limits, fostering a lifestyle that is both fulfilling and responsible.

1.1 Mindful Consumption

- Reduce, Reuse, Recycle: Minimise waste by prioritising reusable products, repairing items, and recycling materials.
- Choose products with minimal environmental impact, such as those made from renewable resources, ethically sourced, or produced with low carbon footprints.
- Adopt a minimalist lifestyle by focusing on quality over quantity, reducing unnecessary possessions, and avoiding overconsumption.

1.2 Sustainable Food Systems

- Reduce your consumption of meat and dairy in favour of plant-based foods, which have a lower environmental impact.
- Support local farmers and opt for organic produce to minimise the carbon footprint associated with food transportation and chemical use.
- Plan meals, store food properly, and compost organic waste to minimise food waste.

1.3 Social Equity

- Social equity ensures that all individuals, regardless of their background, have fair access to resources, opportunities, and rights.
- Ensure equitable access to quality education for children and adults.
- Address food insecurity by supporting community gardens, food banks, and programmes that provide healthy, affordable food to low-income families.

- Ensure that all communities, especially those disproportionately affected by pollution and climate change, have access to clean air, water, and green spaces.
- Promote affordable and accessible healthcare services, including mental health support, for all community members.

2. Core Principles

Neo-ethical Living is a transformative approach that integrates interconnectedness, equality, sustainability, and responsibility into every aspect of life. By building around these four pillars, individuals and communities can create a more just, equitable, and sustainable world. This approach not only addresses the urgent challenges of our time but also fosters a more profound sense of purpose, connection, and ethical responsibility in our daily lives.

2.1 Interconnectedness

At its core, Neo-ethical Living recognises the profound interconnection between humans, other living beings, and the environment. It promotes a sense of responsibility that transcends individual gain, fostering collective well-being and environmental stewardship. American astrophysicist and author Neil deGrasse Tyson (b. 1958) beautifully captures the essence of interconnectedness, reminding us that our existence is deeply intertwined with all life, the planet, and the cosmos. It encourages us to think beyond ourselves and recognise the profound relationships that bind us to each other and the natural world. He says, "We are all connected; To each other, biologically. To the earth, chemically. To the rest of the universe, atomically."

2.2 Equality

A commitment to empathy lies at the core of Neo-ethical Living. This principle encourages understanding others' perspectives, regardless of cultural, social, or economic differences, and acting with compassion to address inequality and injustice. Economic inequality is not only a moral issue but also a practical one, as it can hinder economic progress and social stability. It calls for a more equitable financial system that benefits everyone, not just a privileged few. French politician Christine Lagarde (b. 1956), who has been the President of the European Central Bank since 2019, says, "Inequality is not just morally unacceptable; it is also economically inefficient. It undermines growth, destabilises societies, and hampers the fight against poverty."

2.3 Sustainability

Neo-ethical Living values sustainability as a means to ensure future generations inherit a habitable planet. It integrates environmental conservation, resource efficiency, and a shift toward renewable energy into its ethical framework. There is a powerful Native American proverb saying, "We do not inherit the earth from our ancestors; we borrow it from our children." This beautifully encapsulates the essence of sustainability by reminding us that our actions today have long-term consequences for future generations. It calls for responsible stewardship of the planet, ensuring that we leave a healthy and thriving environment for future generations. Former Harley-Davidson CEO Jochen Zeitz (b. 1963), who served as Puma CEO for 18 years, has relentlessly put sustainability at the heart of his business, shifting the perspective on sustainability from simply reducing negative impacts to actively creating positive change. He says, "Sustainability is no longer about doing less harm. It's about doing more good."

2.4 Responsibility

Neo-ethical Living calls for individual actions that align with broader societal and environmental goals. Energy consumption can be reduced at the personal level by using energy-efficient appliances, LED lighting, and turning off unused electronics. Individuals can minimise waste sent to landfills, reduce the demand for new raw materials, support circular economy initiatives, and reduce the environmental impact of resource extraction and waste management. By buying ethically manufactured products, people can encourage businesses to adopt ethical practices and support global efforts to eradicate poverty and exploitation. Demand on municipal water supplies and promoting sustainable water management are also done at the individual level. By making conscious choices in daily life, individuals can contribute to global efforts to achieve sustainability, equality, and interconnectedness. These actions, when multiplied across communities and nations, have the power to drive systemic change and create a more just, equitable, and sustainable world.

3. A Four-Dimensional Ethical System

3.1 Personal Ethics

This pillar focuses on individual behaviour and lifestyle choices. It encompasses mindful consumption, self-reflection, and cultivating healthy relationships that promote personal and communal growth.

- Adopt a minimalist lifestyle to reduce overconsumption.
- Practise gratitude and mindfulness to foster a sense of contentment and reduce materialistic desires.

- Engage in regular self-assessment to identify areas for ethical improvement.

3.2 Social Ethics

Neo-ethical Living emphasises social equity, inclusivity, and justice. It encourages policies and behaviours that uplift marginalised communities, dismantle systemic inequities, and create opportunities for all.

- Volunteer for or donate to organisations that address social justice issues (for example, poverty, homelessness, education).
- Advocate for policies that promote equality and inclusion in your workplace, school, or community.
- Build strong, supportive relationships and networks that uplift others.

3.3 Environmental Ethics

A cornerstone of Neo-ethical Living, environmental ethics advocates for a harmonious relationship between humans and nature. This includes practices such as reducing waste, conserving resources, and protecting biodiversity.

- Reduce, reuse, and recycle to minimise waste and resource consumption.
- Support sustainable agriculture by choosing organic, locally sourced, and plant-based foods.
- Advocate for policies that protect natural habitats, reduce pollution, and promote the use of renewable energy.

3.4 Technological Ethics

In navigating a world increasingly shaped by technological advancements, Neo-ethical Living incorporates ethical considerations for artificial intelligence, data privacy, and automation. It seeks to ensure technology serves humanity responsibly and equitably.

- Use technology mindfully, avoiding overconsumption of digital resources and e-waste.
- Support ethical tech companies that prioritise user privacy, data security, and environmental sustainability.
- Advocate for policies that regulate harmful technologies (such as surveillance and AI bias) and promote ethical innovation.

This four-dimensional ethical system would provide a robust framework for moral decision-making. Its strength lies in its interconnectedness. Each dimension influences and reinforces the others, creating a holistic approach to ethical living. This system encourages individuals to think holistically, recognising that ethical living is not just about personal choices but also about their broader implications for society, the environment, and technological progress. By considering the impact of our actions across these dimensions, we can create a more just, sustainable, and interconnected world.

4. Application and Action

Neo-ethical Living is a practical, actionable framework that empowers individuals, communities, and organisations to live in alignment with ethical principles. By integrating interconnectedness, equality, sustainability, and responsibility into daily life, we can create a more just, equitable, and sustainable world. It's not just about thinking ethically—it's about acting ethically in every decision we make. Through these practices, we can collectively build a future that respects both people and the planet.

4.1 Integrating Neo-Ethical Practices into Daily Life

- Choose products that are fair trade (equality), eco-friendly (sustainability), ethically produced (responsibility), and locally sourced (interconnectedness).
- Use public transit or carpool (sustainability), support electric vehicle infrastructure (responsibility), and advocate for accessible transportation for all (equality).
- Promote diversity and inclusion (equality), implement green practices (sustainability), take ethical responsibility in decision-making, and foster a collaborative culture (interconnectedness).
- Participate in local initiatives (interconnectedness), support social justice movements (equality), advocate for environmental policies (sustainability), and take personal responsibility for community well-being.

4.2 Scaling Up

Neo-ethical Living isn't just for individuals—it can also guide organisations and governments toward more ethical practices.

- Adopt corporate social responsibility (CSR) initiatives that prioritise sustainability, fair labour practices, and community engagement.

- Implement policies that promote social equity, environmental protection, and ethical governance.
- Teach students about global interconnectedness, social justice, and sustainability, and encourage them to take responsibility for their actions.

5. Challenges and Opportunities

Neo-ethical Living faces several challenges, including resistance to change, economic barriers, and conflicts between individual and collective interests. However, it also opens up opportunities for innovation, collaboration, and transformative societal progress.

5.1 Challenges

There are educational gaps that hinder the widespread adoption of ethical principles. There are economic systems that prioritise short-term gains over long-term sustainability. And there are cultural differences that complicate the creation of universally accepted moral standards. American talk show host Oprah Winfrey (b. 1954) says so aptly, "Challenges are gifts that force us to search for a new centre of gravity. Don't fight them. Just find a new way to stand."

5.2 Opportunities

Some technologies facilitate sustainable practices. Fostering global cooperation is possible to address shared challenges such as climate change. Internet platforms can be used for ethical dialogue and education to build consensus around Neo-ethical principles. American businessman Mark Zuckerberg (b. 1984), who co-founded the social media service Facebook and runs its parent company Meta Platforms, articulates best when he says,

"The biggest risk is not taking any risk. In a world that's changing quickly, the only strategy that is guaranteed to fail is not taking risks."

6. A Vision for Harmony, Empowerment, and Equity

Neo-ethical Living envisions a world where harmony reigns between humanity and nature, where technology empowers rather than exploits, and where individuals contribute to the greater good without losing their autonomy. It seeks to transform the way societies approach development, prioritise equity, and respect the planet.

6.1 The Core Principles of Neo-Ethical Living

Neo-ethical Living is built on four foundational pillars: interconnectedness, equality, sustainability, and responsibility. These principles are not abstract ideals, but actionable guidelines that can reshape how individuals, communities, and societies interact with one another and the planet.

Interconnectedness recognises that all life forms, ecosystems, and human societies are deeply interdependent. It calls for a shift from individualism to a collective mindset, where actions are taken with consideration of their broader impact on people, nature, and future generations.

The equality principle emphasizes fairness, inclusion, and justice. It challenges systemic inequalities and promotes equal access to opportunities, resources, and rights for all individuals, regardless of their background or identity.

The sustainability principle prioritises the long-term health of the planet. It advocates for practices that meet present needs without compromising the ability of future generations to meet theirs, ensuring that development is balanced with environmental stewardship.

The responsibility principle underscores the ethical obligation of individuals, organisations, and governments to act in ways that promote the well-being of people and the planet. It calls for accountability, ethical decision-making, and proactive efforts to address global challenges.

6.2 Harmony Between Humanity and Nature

One of the central tenets of Neo-ethical Living is the restoration of harmony between humanity and nature. For too long, human activities have been driven by exploitation and short-term gains, leading to deforestation, pollution, climate change, and biodiversity loss. Neo-ethical Living seeks to reverse this trend by fostering a deep respect for the natural world and recognising that human well-being is inextricably linked to the health of the planet.

In this envisioned world, sustainable practices become the norm. Individuals and communities adopt lifestyles that minimise environmental impact, such as reducing waste, conserving energy, and supporting local, organic agriculture. Governments and corporations prioritise green technologies and circular economies, where resources are reused and recycled rather than discarded. Biodiversity is protected, and natural habitats are restored, ensuring that ecosystems can thrive. This harmony is not just about preserving nature for its own sake but about creating a symbiotic relationship where humanity benefits from nature's abundance while also nurturing and protecting it. In this world, forests are not just carbon sinks but sacred spaces that inspire awe and reverence. Rivers are not just sources of water but lifelines that connect communities and ecosystems.

6.3 Technology as a Force for Empowerment

In the Neo-ethical Living paradigm, technology is not a tool of exploitation but a force for empowerment. The digital age has brought immense innovation potential, but it has also exacerbated inequalities, invaded privacy, and contributed to environmental degradation. Neo-ethical Living envisions a world where technology is used ethically and responsibly to enhance human well-being and protect the planet.

In this world, renewable energy technologies such as solar, wind, and geothermal power are replacing fossil fuels, thereby reducing greenhouse gas emissions and mitigating climate change. Smart cities use technology to optimise resource use, reduce waste, and improve the quality of life for residents. Artificial intelligence and big data are harnessed to solve complex global challenges, from healthcare to food security, while ensuring that these technologies are transparent, equitable, and free from bias. Moreover, Neo-ethical Living emphasises digital inclusion, ensuring that all individuals, regardless of their socioeconomic status, have access to the benefits of technology. In this world, technology is not a privilege but a right, empowering individuals to learn, connect, and thrive.

6.4 Contributing to the Greater Good Without Losing Autonomy

A key challenge of modern society is balancing individual autonomy with collective responsibility. Neo-ethical Living addresses this by fostering a culture where individuals contribute to the greater good without sacrificing their freedom or identity. It recognises that true autonomy is not about isolation but about making conscious, ethical choices that benefit both the individual and the community.

In this world, individuals are empowered to take personal responsibility for their actions, understanding that their choices have ripple effects on others and the planet. They are encouraged to engage in community building, volunteerism, and advocacy, but they do so out of a sense of purpose and fulfilment rather than obligation. Neo-ethical Living also promotes mindful consumption, where individuals choose products and services that align with their values. They support businesses that prioritise fair labour practices, environmental sustainability, and social responsibility, knowing that their purchasing power can drive positive change. At the same time, Neo-ethical Living respects diversity and individuality. It does not impose a one-size-fits-all approach but encourages people to find their own unique ways of contributing to the greater good. Whether through art, science, activism, or everyday acts of kindness, individuals are free to express their values and talents in ways that resonate with them.

6.5 Transforming Societal Approaches to Development

Neo-ethical Living calls for a fundamental transformation in how societies approach development. Instead of prioritising economic growth at all costs, it advocates for holistic development that balances financial, social, and environmental well-being. In this vision, equity becomes a central focus of development. Governments and organisations work to reduce income inequality, ensure access to education and healthcare, and create opportunities for all individuals to thrive. Sustainable development goals guide policies and practices, ensuring that progress does not come at the expense of the planet or future generations. Neo-ethical Living also challenges the consumerist culture that drives overconsumption and waste. It promotes a shift toward sufficiency and well-being, where individuals find fulfilment in relationships, experiences, and purpose rather than material possessions.

7. A Call to Action

Neo-ethical Living is not a distant utopia but a call to action for individuals, communities, and societies to rethink their values and practices. It envisions a world where harmony between humanity and nature is restored, where technology empowers rather than exploits, and where individuals contribute to the greater good without losing their autonomy. To achieve this vision, we must embrace the principles of interconnectedness, equality, sustainability, and responsibility in our daily lives. We must advocate for policies and practices that prioritise equity and environmental stewardship. We must utilise our creativity, innovation, and compassion to construct a world that is not only prosperous but also just, sustainable, and fulfilling. In the words of Mahatma Gandhi, "The future depends on what you do today." Neo-ethical Living invites us to act today—in our homes, communities, and societies—to create a future where harmony, empowerment, and equity reign. It is a vision worth striving for, not just for us but for generations to come. As Dr APJ Abdul Kalam said, "We are all born with a divine fire in us." Let us ignite that fire to create a world where humanity and nature coexist in harmony, where technology empowers rather than exploits, and where every individual has the opportunity to thrive. By embracing Kalam's wisdom, we can make the planet more liveable for all.

8. Summary

The framework of Neo-ethical Living is a call to action for individuals and communities to embrace ethical principles that are both adaptable and sustainable. By fostering interconnectedness, compassion, and responsibility, it provides a roadmap for navigating the complexities of the modern world while protecting the fundamental values of humanity and the environment. In adopting this framework, we take a crucial step toward creating a future that is not only viable but thriving for generations to come.

9. Conclusion

Neo-Ethical Living is not just about making better choices for us, but about creating a ripple effect that inspires collective responsibility for the planet and future generations. It's where mindfulness meets action, and sustainability becomes a way of life, making the world a more liveable place.

About the Author

Arun Tiwari is a distinguished Indian missile scientist, engineer, professor, and author whose career spans both the frontiers of defence technology and the landscape of inspirational literature. He is best known worldwide as the close associate and co-author of Dr A.P.J. Abdul Kalam, the former President of India, on the iconic autobiography *Wings of Fire*. Tiwari's life embodies a rare confluence: the rigour of scientific innovation, the art of storytelling, and a commitment to using knowledge for human upliftment.

Born in 1955 in Meerut, he graduated with a master's degree in mechanical engineering from GB Pant University. He joined the Defence Research and Development Organisation (DRDO) in 1982, working under Dr Kalam in the Integrated Guided Missile Development Programme (IGMDP). Over the next two decades, he played a pivotal role in creating indigenous hardware systems for the Trishul and Akash surface-to-air missiles, particularly in the development of advanced aluminium alloys and titanium technologies. His work established him as a key contributor to India's quest for self-reliance in strategic defence.

But Tiwari's legacy extends far beyond the laboratory. His career is marked by a belief that technology must ultimately serve society. In the mid-1990s, he collaborated with renowned cardiologist Dr B. Soma Raju to develop the country's first low-cost coronary implant—the Kalam-Raju Stent—an achievement that earned him the prestigious Defence Technology Spin-Off Award. Later, he pioneered telemedicine applications and helped shape the initial phase of the Pan-Africa e-Network, bringing the benefits of broadband connectivity to remote healthcare.

Alongside his technical contributions, Tiwari has built an extraordinary literary body of work. Beyond *Wings of Fire*, his books explore the intersections of science, spirituality, leadership, and social change. He has also published the essence of the great Indian scriptures in English, making timeless wisdom accessible to contemporary readers worldwide. His writings often return to a central theme: that behind all technology, knowledge, and creativity lies the enigma of manifestation—the real intelligence of the cosmos—which works silently through human beings and reveals itself in flashes of discovery, compassion, and service.

His voice reaches further through his digital presence: since 2019, his fortnightly blog (aruntiwari.com) has been widely read, offering reflections on current events, innovation, and philosophy. Through these writings, he has come to be regarded as a "spiritual rationalist"—a thinker who balances mysticism with scientific clarity. Teaching at the University of Hyderabad for a decade as an Adjunct Professor at the School of Management Studies, he developed a renowned course on Medical Humanities for MBA students.

As a teacher, speaker, and author, Arun Tiwari continues to bridge the worlds of technology and human aspiration. His journey—from missiles to medicine, scriptures to cyberspace—underscores a singular truth: that the greatest intelligence is not what we create, but what is revealed through us, in the quiet miracle of manifestation itself.

Books by Arun Tiwari

Published by Sakal Publications

- The Baton Should Not Fall
- Decoding the Pandemic
- India Wakes : Post Coronavirus New World Order
- Innovate Locally to Win Globally
- Live for a Legacy
- Uddhava Gita
- Discovery of Anugita
- Simple Spirituality : Recalling Kabir
- A Modern Interpretation of Tulsidas Ramcharitramanas
- A Modern Interpretation of Lokmanya Tilak's Gita Rahasya
- We are What We Eat
- Yoga Vasishtha
- Spectrum
- Purpose of Life